Teaching Beginning Reading

A
Balanced
Approach

by

Linda Mele Johnson

Fearon Teacher Aids
A Division of Frank Schaffer Publications, Inc.

Senior Editor: Kristin Eclov
Copyeditor: Cindy Barden
Illustrators: Nancee McClure, Becky Radtke, Chris Nye and Janet Skiles
Cover and Inside Design: Good Neighbor Press, Inc. Grand Junction, CO
Cover Photograph: Anthony Nex Photography
© **Fearon Teacher Aids**
A Division of Frank Schaffer Publications, Inc.
23740 Hawthorne Boulevard
Torrance, CA 90505-5927

FE7948
ISBN 1-56417-948-6

789

Table of Contents

Unit I

Target Word Recognition Skills: /ă/, /b/, /m/, /s/, ēe, <u>the</u>, I 1

Unit II

Target Word Recognition Skills: /ŏ/, /c/, /t/, /n/, /d/, /f/, <u>a</u>, Is 32

Unit III

Target Word Recognition Skills: /p/, /r/, /h/, /l/, /g/, /ĭ/, <u>said</u>, <u>of</u>, <u>to</u>, <u>go</u>, <u>as</u>, <u>if</u> 65

Unit IV

Target Word Recognition Skills: /ĕ/, /j/, /k/, /g/, /w/, /x/, /y/, /z/, ē, <u>are</u>, <u>saw</u>, <u>you</u>, <u>won't</u>, <u>have</u>, <u>these</u> 96

Unit V

Target Word Recognition Skills: sh, wh, ch, th, ŭ, <u>my</u>, <u>come</u>, <u>do</u>, <u>they</u>, <u>want</u>, <u>put</u>, <u>what</u>, <u>here</u>, <u>good</u>, <u>hello</u>, OK, <u>don't</u> 148

Table of Contents

Unit VI

Target Word Recognition Skills: ay (pay), o-e (home), ōw (show), ow (now), i-e (kite), _y (fly), ed (want<u>ed</u>), kn (know), ai (tail), ea (eat), ew (grew), <u>one</u>, <u>know</u>, <u>some</u>, <u>more</u>, <u>your</u>, <u>goes</u>, <u>was</u>, <u>or</u>, <u>other</u>, <u>been</u>, <u>would</u>, <u>mother</u>, <u>two</u>

Unit VII

Target Word Recognition Skills: u (found), /ī/ (find), ar (far), /s/ c (pencil), /ng/ (long), _all, _ank, _ink, _ing, <u>there</u>, <u>friends</u>, <u>Mr.</u>, <u>any</u>, <u>from</u>, <u>where</u>, <u>work</u>, <u>little</u>, <u>Father</u>, <u>word</u>, <u>were</u>, <u>find</u>

Unit VIII

Target Word Recognition Skills: _ake, _old, squ_, _y (funny), ir, _igh, ōo (moon) aw, au (all, saw) air, _ly (happily), _le (bubble), wr_, oi, oy, <u>once</u>, <u>upon</u>, <u>bread</u>, <u>who</u>, <u>could</u>, <u>would</u>, <u>again</u>, <u>talk</u>, <u>walk</u>, <u>very</u>, <u>happy</u>, <u>through</u>, <u>noise</u>, <u>thought</u>, <u>were</u>, <u>buy</u>, <u>many</u>, <u>pull</u>, <u>because</u>

Introduction

Why This Book Was Written

Last year while I was attending a reading conference, I met young teachers who complained that their universities had not prepared them to teach beginning reading. They added that the available books and manuals were so convoluted that they found them difficult to follow. These teachers wanted a very practical handbook explaining how to teach beginning reading skills in a sequential and systematic manner.

It is for these teachers, and others to come, that this book was written. I hope it will prove helpful to novice teachers or to any teachers who want a basic resource for teaching beginning reading.

What is Reading?

Simply stated, reading is getting meaning from written text. However simple the definition is, the process of reading is extremely complex, much like thinking itself. During the act of reading, the brain must do many things, quickly and simultaneously.

Think of all the things you need to do when you learn to understand, read, and write in another language. You have to:

- learn the language, at least enough for the reading task at hand.
- "crack the written code"; that is, learn what the symbols represent.
- have enough background knowledge to comprehend the text.

Basically, this is what our students need to be able to do in order to read and write in English.

Beginning reading refers to getting meaning from simple text. Since this text is far below the listening comprehension of the learner, comprehension is mostly related at this beginning level to rapid, effortless word recognition. For this reason, word recognition is stressed in many beginning reading programs. It is the focus of this book because I believe it is crucial to comprehension at this earliest stage of literacy.

What Is A Balanced Approach to Beginning Reading?

I like to think of a balanced approach to reading as one that best simulates the way a child learns to read in an ideal environment. This ideal process begins at birth and proceeds through the following stages:

- The infant hears the sounds of language. Soon the child begins to communicate in the tongue of his or her parents or caregivers.

- The baby who is read to frequently begins to realize that the book holds a message. Soon the child can hold the book upright, start from the beginning and turn the pages.

- The toddler begins to memorize text, asking that the same book be read over and over again.

- The young child plays with language; he or she recites rhymes, sings songs and engages in word play. The child begins to recognize his or her own name as well as those of his or her siblings. The child develops a small sight vocabulary (McDonald's, stop, etc.).

- Soon the child (usually between the ages of four and six) begins to show an interest in the alphabetic system. The child ask lots of questions about letters and their sounds and wants to play at writing and reading. If the child has a strong auditory ability, he or she might begin to "sound out" words on his or her own, asking an adult or older child for verification. If the child is an analytic, visual learner, he or she might first develop a large sight vocabulary and then begin to generalize. For example, the child might remember the word <u>cat</u> and generalize to decode <u>rat</u>, <u>sat</u>, and <u>hat</u>. This child appears to learn "by sight" but has actually internalized the sound system by going from the whole word to the parts.

A "balanced approach" takes the child at his or her appropriate level. The wise teacher will begin instruction with the child's background of experiences firmly in mind. For example, if the child is just learning English, the teacher should stress English language development while introducing written language during "experience story" time. Formal decoding instruction should not begin until the student has at least a working knowledge of English (Score of 4 or 5 on a Language Assessment Scale). If there is a teacher who is proficient in the native language of the child, decoding can begin in the child's own language. These skills will transfer to English. A child who is literate in his or her own language always has an advantage over one who is not.

Students who are fluent in English but have had few book experiences at home would also benefit from several months of language, alphabet and phonemic awareness practice before proceeding to formal reading lessons.

Most children arrive in first grade at stage 5. For those with excellent auditory and visual memory, reading tasks will be easy. These children will probably internalize the rules of written English within a few months.

Approximately 1/3 of any class I have ever taught has been in this category. For the most part

these are the students who would learn with any approach, but they can be "turned off" by too much skills instruction that is not needed. There are legions of horror stories about fluent six-year olds who were forced to spend first grade going through the same beginning reading programs as their less experienced peers. The teacher must be very aware of the serious results of such miseducation, as they can have lasting effects on a child's attitude toward reading. The last thing any teacher or parent would want to see is an eager, competent reader turned into a reluctant one.

The teacher will discover that the majority of the students in her first grade class need support in language development as well as explicit instruction in word attack (decoding) skills. An approach that combines the best of holistic methods with an explicit, systematic skills program is what is meant by a "balanced program." This is the approach used in this book.

How to Use This Book

The purpose of this book is to provide you, the teacher, with suggestions for systematically teaching beginning reading using a variety of supplemental materials and reading programs. It is a fact, that not every teacher has access to the same supplemental reading materials. Some schools may be using Houghton Mifflin, some Rigby, and others Scholastic, Modern Curriculum Press, or The Wright Group. The author has evaluated a variety of supplemental materials and has recommended specific titles that reinforce the skills presented in each lesson.

Teaching Beginning Reading: A Balanced Approach is organized into eight units with a total of 62 individual lessons. Each unit teaches specific skills which are then reinforced throughout the lessons.

Lesson Overview

Teaching examples and explanations for how to use each section are provided as a reference.

Each lesson is presented in the following format:

Sight Vocabulary

    Phonics

    Spelling

    Grammar, Mechanics, and Usage

    Developing Phonemic Awareness

        Read Aloud

        Shared Reading

            Books

            Rhymes and Poems

            Songs

Direct Instruction

    Working With Letters and Sounds

    Blend, Read, and Write

    Word Construction

Books to Enhance Reading Comprehension, Skill and Language Development

    Guided Reading

    Independent Reading

    Writing Frame

    Make Your Own Little Books

    Letter Cards for Word Construction

    Word Cards for Sentence Construction

Sight Vocabulary

"Sight words" are words frequently found in English text. These words are often irregular in spelling and should be instantly recognized at the earliest possible time. Sight words are introduced and then reviewed throughout the lessons. Children are given many opportunities to recognize the sight words in text and use them in their writing activities. For a list of sight words, see page 414.

Phonics Instruction

Phonics instruction can be both analytic and synthetic. In an analytic approach, the teacher encourages and teaches the child to look at the whole word as a means to understanding its parts or generalizing it to other words. For example, if the child knows the word "all" he or she can be shown how to make the words ball, call, and tall. If the child comes across the unknown word "trudge," the teacher might say "Think of fudge."

In a synthetic approach, the teacher instructs the child to join phonemes together to make whole words. For example, /c/-/a/-/t/ = cat.

Every practitioner knows that readers (adults as well as children) use both analytic and synthetic approaches depending upon the particular circumstances or learning styles. The more experienced a reader is, the more he or she tends to resort to an analytic approach to decoding an unknown word. Beginners and veterans alike, when confronted by a word that does not fit a pattern in his or her memory bank, will resort to a synthetic approach. For example, if I saw the name "Blance" I'd immediately rhyme it with "chance" because that is the pattern in my mind. If I saw something like "Rysenthalitsky" I'd probably start at the beginning of the word, look carefully at all the letters and try to "sound it out." The synthetic approach to decoding is stressed in this book because it helps the beginner with the critical concept that letters represent spoken sounds and can be arranged sequentially to represent the spoken word. A child who does not understand this concept will not be able to analyze words effectively because he or she does not yet know that a word is made up of parts. For example, you cannot ask Juan to substitute the letter "c" for the letter "b" at the beginning of the word "bake" if he doesn't know the word has a beginning!

VII

It is important to remember that these phonics lessons should be short, fun, appropriate and meaningful.

Spelling

(Faye Bolton and Diane Snowball, <u>Ideas for Spelling</u>, Portsmouth: Heinemann, 1993.) In my opinion, spelling should be taught daily, within the context of direct instruction and writing. Mastery of lists of words and spelling tests are inappropriate at this early stage, but the teacher will have to respond to the needs and desires of her students, their parents, and perhaps even the principal.

I have found that children remember high frequency words (the, is, to) best if I ask them to help me spell during a shared writing activity.

Here is an example of a spelling activity that I have found to be very successful. (By "successful" I mean the children use the correct spelling in their own independent writing.)

Teacher: We've had quite a day today. What shall we write in our class journal? (Teacher has large spiral chart.)

Child: We went to the zoo!

Teacher: Yes. Let's write that down. How do you spell "we"?

Children: w-e

Teacher: Right. Capital <u>w</u> because it is the first word in the sentence. Let's not forget a space. Now how do we spell "went"?

Child: w-a-n-t

Teacher: e e eeelephant, weeent

Child: w-e-n-t

Teacher: Good. To?

Child: t-o

Teacher: Good. The?

Children: t-h-e

Teacher: You are getting so good at this. How about "zoo"?

Children: z-o-o!

Teacher: Yes—and what do I put at the end?

Children: A period.

Teacher: Right. It's the end of our sentence.

Phonetically regular words are taught during daily phonics lessons.

The teacher should encourage children to use conventional spellings for words that have been introduced (display these words in the classroom, perhaps, on a "Word Wall" or word collection) and "temporary" or approximate spelling for other words.

[**TIP!** Parents sometimes misunderstand the term "invented" spelling, but none has ever complained about "temporary" spelling for a six year old.]

Grammar, Mechanics and Usage

I teach grammar, mechanics, and usage in the context of writing activities, both formal and informal. Here's an example:

Child: Teacher, I lost a tooth! (Much excitement from everyone, especially if blood is shed!)

Teacher: Oh, my! Let's get an envelope to put it in. (Gets envelope and carefully places tooth in it). I'll write: "Elvia's tooth" on the envelope because the tooth belongs to Elvia. Let's spell Elvia's name.

Children: Capital E-l-v-i-a

Teacher: We need to add apostrophe "s" to show that the tooth belongs to Elvia. It is Elvia's tooth.

Developing Phonemic Awareness

According to Marilyn Jager Adams, the discovery of the importance of phonemic awareness in learning to read might be the most important breakthrough in our understanding of reading methodology in this century. (See Marilyn Jager Adams, Beginning to Read, Cambridge: MIT, 1995.)

Phonemic awareness is the understanding that letters represent individual sounds (phonemes) in spoken language. Without this understanding, phonics instruction will make little sense to the child and spelling will be learned through memorization.

A child who has phonemic awareness can rhyme words, engage in phonetic word play, and give the letters that represent sounds at the beginning, middle or end of a word. If the teacher gives a child the word all, he or she can easily construct the words ball, call, fall, hall and small, at first orally, and later in writing.

Research tells us that phonemic awareness is critical to success in beginning reading. (Stanovich, 1986, 1993, Share and Stanovich, 1995, Adams, 1995.)

Phonemic awareness develops over the course of many years; indeed it probably begins at the moment an adult says "Kitchy Kitchy Koo" to an infant. There are many things the classroom teacher can do to support this developing process in kindergarten and grade one: (Ideas adapted from Teaching Reading, California Department of Education, 1996.)

- Recite many poems and rhymes, drawing attention to individual words and sounds.
- Sing many songs, tracking and pointing to individual words and letters. A great song for this is "Willoughby Wallaby Woo", sung by Raffi. (See Raffi, Singable Songs for the Very Young. Words by Dennis Lee, Homeland Publishing, 1976)

- Engage the children in humorous word plays:
  "Eeny, meeny, miny moo
  a tiger ran after you!"

Don't be afraid to make these silly rhymes up to correspond with the names of your students. I guarantee the kids will think you're great!

- Recite tongue twisters.
- Substitute initial consonant sounds to make new words (Jill, hill, Bill.)
- Listen for and identify the sounds that come at the beginning, the middle and the ends of words.
- Write the letters that you hear in words spoken orally (duck, hat, ham)
- Blend sounds together to make words (sssaaat) and segment sounds in words (sat is /s/ /a/ /t/).
- Clap the number of syllables in a word.

Until a child demonstrates phonemic awareness, he or she will make little progress in reading or spelling. For the child who has yet to develop this important ability, spend lots of time on the above listed activities, while building a sight word vocabulary through language experience stories. Phonics instruction will be of little use until the child demonstrates his or her understanding of the basic concepts that support this kind of learning. Until a child has phonemic awareness, he or she will not profit from phonics instruction.

Read Aloud

Reading aloud to children is one of the most important things a parent or teacher can do to develop a high degree of competence and a love for reading. This is because these books, which should always be chosen for their excellence and relevance to children's lives, are way above the child's present reading ability. They provide the vocabulary and background knowledge that become so critical to comprehension once the child is beyond the "crack the code" phase. Also, if the books are chosen with utmost care (the teacher should love them too) the child will develop a love for reading that will stay for the rest of his or her life. Never skip read aloud time.

Shared Reading

Shared reading books are books that are read together (teacher and students). They can be big books, poems or songs that are read chorally or little books that can be easily memorized by the child. There are many advantages to shared reading:

- The child has the opportunity to read and enjoy an entire text. This builds confidence and love for reading.

- The child practices many readiness skills: left-to-right directionality, "tracking words," discussing story, predicting outcomes, etc.

- The child has the opportunity to see sight vocabulary words many, many times.

- The child has the opportunity to learn and apply many skills within a meaningful context.

- Children who are holistic learners will learn to read simply by sharing books with an adult. These children internalize the rules of written language without much direct instruction. Many of these children come from print-rich backgrounds but not always.

- Many "direct instruction" lessons can be based on shared reading activities, thereby giving the lesson the all-important meaningful context. For example:

    Teacher: Boys and Girls, today when we read the nursery rhyme "I Had a Little Nut Tree" Raul noticed that Lisettes's name starts with "L." I'm really happy he saw this because today we are going to learn about the letter "L."

    (Teacher proceeds with direct instruction).

Shared reading also provides opportunities for teaching many skills in context. For example:

Teacher: Look at this. [points to text that says "Jack's mother was angry."] Does anyone notice anything about this?

Child: That's like what you wrote when Ana lost a tooth.

Teacher: Yes. Remember yesterday I wrote "Ana's tooth" on the envelope. Here it says "Jack's mother" because the mother belongs to Jack. Jack's name is spelled with an "apostrophe s" to show that it is Jack's mother.

Direct Instruction

Research tells us that direct instruction is an essential component in a beginning reading program. Although many children do learn how to read from informal and incidental instruction, most do not. Every day I incorporate whole class and small group instruction into my language arts program. The novice teacher might wish to stay with "whole class" instruction until she feels confident enough to work with small groups.

In general, I use a format for teaching direct instruction based on Madeleine Hunter's, Mastery Teaching (El Segundo, CA: Tip Publications, 1983):

- Gain the attention of the students. Establish standards of behavior.

- Tell the children what they will learn.

- Relate the new learning to something they already know.

- Teach. Use as many multisensory techniques as possible.

- Guide the practice. Give the children practice. Monitor and provide feedback.

- Reteach if necessary.
- Give a follow-up activity for independent work.
- Evaluate. Did the children learn the skill?

Working With Letters and Sounds

I adapted the idea for "soundboxes" from internationally known psychologist and reading expert Marie Clay. (Marie M. Clay, <u>The Early Detection of Reading Difficulties</u>, Heinemann, Third Edition, 1985, 1988.)

This activity is designed for children experiencing difficulty in segmenting sounds within words. These students do not understand what you are talking about when you ask "What sound can you hear in the middle? What sound do you hear at the end? At the beginning?" These are the children who see a word, such as "sun" and say "nice" or "sat." They haven't yet grasped the alphabetic principle of our written language.

It is important for the teacher to be discriminate in her use of "soundbox" activities. A child who has "cracked the code" will find such activities meaningless and boring. The child who needs it, however, will be challenged to see if he or she can put the correct letter in the right box! This technique is a good tool for the child having sound sequencing problems. It also provides good reinforcement for left-to-right directionality and letter formation.

Blend, Read, and Write

In this activity, the children are shown how sounds are blended together to make words. The arrow drawn under the word represents the blending of the sounds. If a letter is silent a dotted line is drawn through it.

Word Construction

Word Construction is an activity designed to reinforce phonics and spelling lessons. Its strength lies in the fact that it is a manipulative activity that is interesting to children. Word construction can be done with cut-up letters, magnetic letters, or letter tiles. Letter cards have been provided in the back of the book for each lesson (starting with Unit I, Lesson 6, on page 300). Word Construction activities can be integrated with handwriting lessons by having the students print their own letters on the extra blank squares of paper. Children can practice writing the appropriate capital letter on the back of each letter card.

Word construction activities can be tailored to suit learners at different stages of development. For the emergent reader, the teacher might guide the children very carefully:

Teacher: Let's make "cat." What do you hear first?

Child: c

Teacher: Right. Let's find the letter "c". Here it is! Have you found yours?

Children: Yes!

Teacher: What's comes next? caaat.

Children: a

Teacher: Yes, let's find it. What's comes at the end? Right, c-a-t, cat.

For "advanced" students*:

Teacher: Find the letters f-a-n-t-a-s-t-i-c. Who knows what it spells?

Child: Fantastic!

Teacher: Right! Now let's see how many words you can make with the letters in "fantastic."

Children: [Make as, is, fan, at, fast, etc.]

(*Pat Cunningham, <u>Making Words</u>, Torrance, CA: Good Apple, 1994.)

Guided Reading

Guided reading is what most of us remember as small group instruction from our own early school years. It is probably the most important part of the reading instructional program because this is when the teacher:

- observes each child closely;
- teaches the child at his or her own instructional level;
- makes decisions regarding the child's future lessons.

A guided reading group should consist of approximately 4-6 children who have similar instructional needs. During instruction, the teacher will do some or all of the following: (For a thorough treatment of this topic, see Guided Reading by Irene Fountas and Gay Su Pinnell, Portsmouth: Heinemann, 1996.)

- Distribute books that are at the group's instructional level (children should be able to read with 90% accuracy).
- Build a background of knowledge to help the reader understand the text.
- Teach or reinforce word attack or comprehension skills needed by the students.
- Support and teach the individual child as he or she reads the text independently.
- Evaluate each child's progress. Was the text too easy? Too difficult? What skills or strategies need to be taught next?
- Choose follow-up or reinforcement activities.

Although I have suggested books for guided reading at the end of each lesson, the teacher must make his or her own selection. Since the whole purpose of guided reading is to support the reading of unknown text that is within the child's capabilities, only the child's teacher is in the position to make a wise choice. (A reproducible reference chart for helping figure out unknown words in text is provided on page 416.)

Here is an example of a guided reading lesson for emergent (beginning) readers who are limited English proficient:

Text: Cat on a Mat by Brian Wildsmith

Purpose of Lesson:

1. To reinforce animal vocabulary.
2. To practice sight words a, the, on.
3. To practice decoding cat, sat, mat.
4. To encourage use of picture cues.
5. To teach meaning of the word mat. (This is the only new information. All other skills have been learned, but practice is needed.)

Building background:

Teacher: Boys and girls, I have brought this red mat from home because today we are going to read about a cat who sat on a mat. Does anyone have one of these at home?

Child: We have a yellow one in our bathroom.

Teacher: Yes, lots of people have mats in their bathrooms. I have one in mine, too.

Child: I have one in front of our door.

Teacher: Does the mat have anything written on it?

Child: I don't know.

Teacher: I saw a mat once that had the word "Welcome" written on it.

Child: That means come in.

Teacher: Yes, you're welcome to come in. I want you to visit me.

Child: What's that? (Pointing to a brown sack).

Teacher: Oh, I'm glad you asked. I have some little toy animals here. I thought you would enjoy putting them on the mat and playing with them later.

Children: Yeah!

Teacher: Who would like to put the toy goat on the mat? (Gives other examples of toy animals. Distributes all of them and allows children to place the animals on the mat.) Okay, we'll put this on the toy shelf. You might want to play with it later.

Guided Reading Activity:

Teacher: Here is the book we're going to read. It is one of my favorites. When you get your copy, take a look at it. (Distributes copies.)

Child: Cat on a Mat!

Teacher: Right! The author/illustrator is Brian Wildsmith.

Child: He's the one from yesterday.

Teacher: You noticed! Good for you. He illustrated the alphabet book I read yesterday. Before you read, what will you remember to do if you come to a word you don't know?

Child: Look at the pictures!

Teacher: Yes, they give us good clues. And?

Child: Start from the beginning.

Teacher: Yes. Any other ideas?

Child: Skip it and read to the end?

Teacher: Good. Anything else?

Child: Look at the letters and make the sounds.

Teacher: Yes, you know a lot of sounds now. Blend them together and see if that works.

Child: It has to make sense!

Teacher: Right! Ok, let's read. (She listens to each child, giving help when needed).

Child: (reading) The cat (?)...

Teacher: Start again.

Child: The cat...

Teacher: Skip and continue.

Child: The cat "blank" on the mat. (Still can't figure it.)

Teacher: (Takes child's finger and moves it slowly under the word <u>sat</u>, elongating the first two sounds <u>sssaaat</u>.)

Child: sat!

Teacher: Good. Start frrom the beginning to see if it makes sense. (To whole group.) How come the cat's alone again in the end?

Child: He scared them.

Teacher: I wonder why?

Child: He wants to be by himself.

Child: Cats are like that.

Teacher: Yes, they are! Did you like this book?

Children: Yes!

Teacher: Why? (Accepts all responses.)

Evaluating:

The teacher notices that several children have trouble remembering the names of the animals, especially "goat." She makes a mental note to choose more books with animals in them. She also notices that all the children had to think before recognizing one or more sight words. She will make up a game to reinforce these words before going on to more difficult text. After dismissing the group, she quickly writes these notes in her plan book.

A word of caution about guided reading. The texts used for these lessons should be decodable; that is the children should be able to read the words with 90% accuracy. I have noticed that some of the new basal readers have stories at the beginning levels that are much too difficult for guided reading lessons. These stories are really for shared reading experiences:

Examples of simple text:

The boy walked to the park.

The girl walked to the park.

The dog walked to the park.

The cat walked to the park.

Examples of difficult text:

The horse trotted.

The snake slithered.

The giraffe stretched.

The turtle crawled.

Independent Reading

Independent reading is a time when children are given the opportunity for free choice reading. To make this important time a success, the teacher should:

- Make sure the classroom is stocked with many interesting, easy books, lists, transparencies, charts, and magazines.

- Encourage the children to select easy books; ones with words that they recognize or can figure out.

- Require the children to read aloud. For example, say "I want to hear everyone's voice."

- Keep a simple record of the books the children have read. They enjoy seeing their progress.

Independent Activities

"What do I do with the other kids while I'm having guided reading?" Every teacher must decide what makes him or her most comfortable, as there are several ways to meet this challenge. This is what I do:

After a whole class lesson, I give an assignment that everyone can do to some extent , such as illustrating sentences, sentence construction (word cards are provided in the back of the book for most lessons), cutting and pasting sentences in the correct order, following written directions. I encourage the children to help each other with this assignment. After the children have completed this seatwork, they are allowed free play (blocks, listening, playhouse, art, writing, library, painting, etc.). This works best for me because the more involved the children are in their own pursuits, the less they will disturb me while I am teaching my small group.

(Note: Most of the time I have a bilingual aide to supervise the children at their seats. When she is absent, I do more whole class instruction.)

Here's a list of recommended centers for independent activities for children to do during guided reading:

Assigned reading and writing activities

Library corner

Listening center

Writing center

Painting

Puzzles, Blocks and Games

Computer

Dramatic Play (playhouse, puppet stage)

Theme-related projects

Easy science experiments

Writing Frames

The writing frames have been provided for the teacher's convenience. However, it is best to plan writing activities around the current interests and experiences of your students.

My Own Little Books

We have included one reproducible little book for each lesson. These books were written to give children little books to read, enjoy, take home and keep. Each little book emphasizes vocabulary and skills introduced in that lesson. The little books have been designed to be reproduced on a single two-sided sheet of paper.

To make little books: cut along the dotted line. Fold each section in half. Then insert one section into the other so that the page numbers are sequential. Staple along the fold. Encourage the children to color their little books and take them home to read with their families.

Letter Cards for Word Construction

These letter cards support the "word construction" activity of the lesson. Letter cards are provided at the back of the book for each lesson (starting with Unit I, Lesson 6, page 300). They are included for the convenience of the teacher, but it is beneficial for the child to write the letters by himself or herself. This reinforces letter recognition and handwriting. If you decide to use the letter cards provided, reproduce a set for each student. Use the blank cards for making additional letters. Children can practice writing capital letters on the back of each letter card. Provide children with manila envelopes or small boxes for storing their letter cards. Encourage the children to use the letter cards to make words.

Word Cards for Sentence Construction

These word cards can be used for a meaningful seatwork or small group activity. Help the child to construct sentences and record the sentences in a notebook or writing journal. Another option is to have the child paste the words at the bottom of an 8 1/2" x 11" (21.3cm x 30cm) sheet of paper. The child can then illustrate his or her sentence.

Evaluation/Assessment

At the end of each unit is a short assessment of word recognition skills. To assess comprehension, the teacher should select unknown text for the child to read. Questioning and miscue analysis should help the teacher plan for that child's future instruction.

To assess a beginner's progress, I usually make up the text myself because I know exactly where the child is. I might write something like this:

Karina is a girl.

She is six years old.

She likes to play.

She plays with Lisette.

Karina and Lisette play on the Big Toy.

Always pull out the child's folder when you take the time to assess him or her, so you'll have good records to review at a later time, or to help with parent conferences and report cards.

As the child reads I do my own version of a "running record" (See Marie Clay, The Early Detection of Reading Difficulties, Third Edition, Heinemann, 1985, 1988) with notations that help me plan appropriate future lessons for the individual student.

Poetry Notebook

Children enjoy reading poems over and over again. It gives them the experience of fluent reading. Provide the children with notebooks for collecting poetry. The carefully selected poems and rhymes referenced in this book can be copied and pasted in the child's poetry notebook. You will be pleased to see your students take these notebooks out again and again during independent reading time.

How it All Works Together

The lessons are intended to be taught throughout an integrated day, or days, depending on the needs of the children. It is important to realize that what works for one teacher will not necessarily work for another. There are many ways to organize the day for instruction, here is just one example:

8:30 - 9:00 Oral Language Activities

"Let's Begin Our Day" oral activities (see page 416)

Shared Reading from Charts and Big Books

Singing and Reciting from Charts and Big Books

9:00 - 9:15 **Independent Reading**

Teacher reads a few "instant readers"

Children read books already introduced

9:15 - 10:15 Math

10:15 - 10:20 Restroom break

10:20 - 10:30 **Direct Instruction** (usually whole class phonics/handwriting/spelling lesson)

10:30 - 10:55 **Guided Reading** (one group)

Teacher calls up small groups (4-6 children) for guided reading and word recognition instruction.

Other children are engaged in **independent activities** that focus on unit of study in science, health or social studies.

10:55 - 11:10 (Recess)

11:10 - 12:10 **Guided Reading** (two groups)
Writing (Teaching in the form of direct instruction, modeled writing, shared writing, interactive writing and independent writing.)

Writing practice

Reading of children's written work

12:10 - 12:45 (Lunch)

12:45 - 1:10 **Read Aloud**

Books are selected to support concepts, skills and units of study being emphasized. Books featuring math concepts are included.

1:10 - 1:30 Physical Education

For children learning English, choose games, songs and exercises emphasizing language.

1:30 - 2:10 Thematic Studies (Health Science, Social Studies). Correlate with all other subjects.

Integrate with language arts as often as possible.

2:10 - 2:20 (Recess)

2:20 - 2:40 "Sharing," Class Journal (Shared and Interactive Writing)

Unit I

Target Word
Recognition
Skills:

/ă/, /b/, /m/, /s/, /ē/, ee,
<u>the</u>, I

Unit 1
Lesson 1

Sight Vocabulary:

■ Introduce: I

Developing Phonemic Awareness

Read Aloud:

A is for Animals - David Pelham (Simon & Schuster)

A is for Astronaut - Sian Tucker (Simon & Schuster)

Annie, Bea and Chi Chi Dolores - Donna Mauer (Houghton Mifflin, Invitation to Literacy)

Shared Reading:

Brown Bear, Brown Bear, What Do You See? - Bill Martin, Jr. (Holt)

The Little Red Hen - Brenda Parkes (Rigby, Big Book)

Rhymes and Poems:

"Little Jumping Joan" - Mother Goose

"I Had a Little Nut Tree" - Mother Goose

"Notice" - David McCord in Ready, Set, Read! (Doubleday)
    Also included in Big Book of Rhymes (Harcourt Brace, Signatures.)

Songs:

"ABC Song" - Greg and Steve in We All Live Together, Volume I
    (Youngheart Records)

"BINGO" - Greg and Steve in We All Live Together, Volume IV
    (Youngheart Records)

"Love Somebody"*

Love somebody, yes I do.

Love somebody, yes I do.

Love somebody, yes I do.

I love _____.

* Sing to the tune of "Skip to My Loo."

Direct Instruction: I

1. Tell the children a story about yourself, starting with the word "I" (I like to go on trips). Say: "I think I'll write that down." Write "I" on the board followed by a picture of what you like to do. Do this several times, framing the word "I."

Unit I
Lesson 1

Example:

2. Pass out large sheets of white paper. Show children how to write "I" in the upper left-hand corner. Direct them to draw and color a picture illustrating what they like to do. As the children are drawing, walk around the room taking the children's dictation.

Example:

. . . like to play.

3. Bind papers together to make a book. Ask children to suggest a title that will tell what the book is about. Let the children watch as you write the title and your room number on the cover.

4. Practice writing "I" using chalkboards, whiteboards or paper (ruled or unruled depending on the needs of the children.) It is very important to monitor correct handling of the pencil, as well as letter formation, as lifelong habits are being formed at this time.

Unit I
Lesson 1

Books to Enhance Reading Comprehension, Skill or Language Development

Guided Reading:
Who Likes Ice Cream? - Andrea Butler (Rigby)

Independent Reading:
wordless picture books

catalogs

magazines

concept books

flip books

novelty books

Activity for Home or School
Make little books. Each page starts with "I" followed by a drawing that completes the child's thought.

Writing Frame:
I _____.

Make Your Own Little Books
Me, pages 5-6. (Book 1)

Tip:
Place the word "I" in a prominent place in the classroom (on a word wall or pocket chart). Do this with each new sight word. Ask children to collect their words in an envelope or box.

Words to Practice

I

8

Me

Name _____

1

I sleep.

6

I walk.

3

I talk.

2

I dream.

7

I eat.

4

I play.

5

Unit 1
Lesson 2

Sight Vocabulary:

- Review <u>I</u>
- Phonics: /ă/

Spelling: I ("capital I")

Grammar, Mechanics and Usage: The period

Developing Phonemic Awareness

Read Aloud:

<u>The Monster Book of ABC Sounds</u> - Alan Snow (Dial)

Shared Reading:

<u>From Acorn to Zoo</u> - Satoshi Kitamura (Scholastic, <u>Literacy Place</u>)

Books - Pupil-made "I" Book (See Activity for Home or School, page 4)

<u>The Gingerbread Man</u> - Brenda Parkes (Rigby, Big Book)

<u>Clap Your Hands</u>. Lorinda Bryan Cauley (Harcourt Brace, <u>Signatures</u>, Big Book)

Rhymes and Poems:

"Pat a Cake" - Mother Goose

"The Fat Cat" - Stephanie Calmenson in <u>Ready, Set, Read!</u> (Doubleday)

"Notice" - David McCord in <u>Big Book of Rhymes</u> (Harcourt Brace, <u>Signatures</u>) Also included in <u>Ready, Set, Read!</u> (Doubleday).

Songs:

"ABC Song" - Greg and Steve in <u>We All Live Together, Volume 1</u> (Youngheart Records)

"Apples and Bananas" - Raffi with Ken Whiteley in <u>One Light, One Sun</u> (MCA)

Direct Instruction: /ă/

1. Point to the lower case "a," Say "This letter stands for the sound "ă" that you hear at the beginning of apple, Ann, and Alex (Use children's names if possible).

2. Run you finger under the "a," saying "ăăăă" as you move from left to right. Hold the sound when your finger is under the "ă." Make one continuous sound.

ă

3. Demonstrate the formation of the letter "Aa." As the children trace onto the carpet with their index and middle fingers, have them make the "ă" sound.

Practice with Language Experience

1. Pass out large sheets of white paper. Show the children how to position the paper <u>vertically</u>. Ask them to draw and color pictures of themselves.

Example:

2. As the children are drawing, walk around the room writing each child's name and the word "and" at the bottom of the paper, emphasizing the beginning sound of "and."

Example:

Vera and . . .

8

**Unit 1
Lesson 2**

3. Put all the pictures together, placing your own at the end. Instead of the word "and" you will use a period. Do this in front of the children, modeling your reasoning. ("This is the end, so I will put a period here.")

Example:

Mrs. Johnson.

4. Bind these papers together. You now have a book of your class. Help the children choose an appropriate title.

Books to Enhance Comprehension, Skill and Language Development

Guided Reading:
Deep in the Forest - Brinton Turkle (Dutton)

Independent Reading:
Add new pupil-made books, Brown Bear, Brown Bear, What Do You See? - Bill Martin, Jr. (Holt) and Who Likes Ice Cream? - Andrea Butler (Rigby)

Writing Frame:
I _____ and _____.

Make Your Own Little Books:
My Five Senses, pages 10-11. (Book 2)

Tip:
Take Polaroid™ pictures of the children doing different things. Have someone take a picture of you. Model a sentence for your own picture, such as, "I teach." Elicit responses from the children and write what they say under their pictures:
I paint.
I talk.
I build with blocks.
Bind these pages together for a book your students will be able to read.

Words to Practice

I

My Five Senses

Name _____

<table>
<tr><td>8</td><td>1</td></tr>
</table>

 -

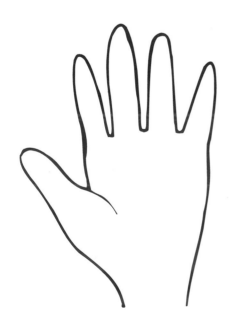

I touch.

I see.

<table>
<tr><td>6</td><td>10
Reproducible</td><td>3</td></tr>
</table>

I taste.
Yum!

2   7

I hear.

I smell.

4

Reproducible

5

Unit I
Lesson 3

Sight Vocabulary:

- Review I
- Phonics: /m/

Spelling: I, am

Grammar, Mechanics and Usage:
Constructing a sentence; questions and answers

Developing Phonemic Awareness

Read Aloud:

Monster Book of ABC Sounds - Alan Snow (Dial)

I Am Five - Louise Fitzhugh (Delacorte)

Whose Mouse Are You? - Robert Kraus (Macmillan)

Where the Wild Things Are - Maurice Sendak (Harper)

On Mother's Lap - Ann Herbert Scott (Houghton Mifflin, Literary
    Readers)

I Am Six - Ann Morris (Silver Press)

Shared Reading:

Lazy Mary - June Melser (Wright Group, Big Book)

Today Is Monday – Eric Carle (Big Book in Scholastic's Literacy Place)

Rhymes and Poems:

"Mary, Mary Quite Contrary" - Mother Goose

"Little Miss Muffet" - Mother Goose

"Mary Had a Little Lamb" - Mother Goose

To Market To Market - (Wright Group, Big Book)

Songs:

"Miss Mary Mack" - Ella Jenkins Nursery Songs (Smithsonian
    Folkways)

Direct Instruction: /m/

1. Say "Who likes ice cream? Who likes cake? Candy? Cookies?" This
   should elicit the sound "mmm" from some of the children, as well as "I
   do" and other responses.

2. Point to the letter "m." Tell the children that this letter stands for
   the sound that many of them have just made. Say "mmm" while
   rubbing your stomach. Invite the children to join you.

Unit I
Lesson 3

3. Show children how "a" and "m" can be put together to make a word.

am

Run you finger from left to right under the word "am". Prolong the sound of each letter, but make sure the sounds are continuous.

ăăămmmm

4. Have children rub their tummies as they make the "m" sound.

5. Model the correct formation of "Mm." Ask the children to practice writing this letter while making the sound it represents.

Practice with Language Experience

1. Surprise the children with Polaroid™ pictures of each of them. Say, "I'll ask you a question. When you answer me, you may have a picture of yourself." Ask: "Who are you?" When a child responds "I am Benji" write this on an 8½" x 11" (21.3cm x 27.5cm) sheet of paper. Ask the children to help you spell. Make sure they can see you as you write.

2. Ask the children to paste the photographs onto their papers. You might want them to trace over the sentence.

3. Bind the pages together for another book.

I am Jennifer.

Working with Letters and Sounds

1. Show children how to make three adjacent squares called soundboxes on their chalkboards or papers.

Point out that the box on their left is the first box, the next is the middle, and the third is the last.

2. Show them how the word "monkey" begins with an "m" so we put the m in the first box.

| m | | |

Tip:
Children enjoy tracing with markers.

Tip:
An understanding of this concept is crucial to the decoding process. Do it with the children until they feel confident. Make sure second language learners understand the vocabulary.

Unit 1
Lesson 3

3. Continue with the word "ham". Since the <u>m</u> is at the end, we put the <u>m</u> in the last box.

		m

4. Do this with the children, using the following words:

mouse	drum	lamb
mother	morning	jam
man	mountain	magic

Books to Enhance Comprehension, Skill and Language Development

Guided Reading:

<u>Monster Mop</u> - Aimee Mark (Modern Curriculum Press, <u>Ready Readers</u>)

<u>What Are You?</u> - Andrea Butler (Rigby)

Independent Reading:

Add pupil-made books

Writing Frame:

I am _____.

Make Your Own Little Books:

<u>Feelings</u>, pages 15-16. (Book 3)

> **Tip:**
> Have each child draw a picture of himself with **black** pen or marker. At the bottom write (or have child trace) "I am Steven." Copy each page and bind together so each child will have a book he can read. . . . or make a single Big Book for the class to share.

Words to Practice

I

am

Feelings

Name _____

8

1

 -

I am angry.

6

I am sad.

3

I am happy.

2

I am glad.

7

 -

I am sorry.

4

I am scared.

5

Unit I
Lesson 4

Sight Vocabulary:

- Review I
- Introduce the
- Phonics: /b/

Spelling: I, the, am

Grammar, Mechanics and Usage:
Questions and answers and corresponding punctuation

Developing Phonemic Awareness

Read Aloud:

Bears - Ruth Kraus (Harper)

Blueberries for Sal - Robert McCloskey (Scholastic)

There's An Alligator under My Bed - Mercer Mayer (Dial)

Buzz, Buzz, Buzz Went Bumblebee - Colin West (Candlewick)

Big Fat Hen - Keith Baker (Harcourt Brace)

When This Box Is Full - Patricia Lillie (Houghton Mifflin, Literary Readers)
   Also included in Scholastic's Literary Place.

Shared Reading:

Goldilocks and the Three Bears - Janet Hillman (Rigby, Big Book)

Poems and Rhymes:

"Baa-Baa Black Sheep" - Mother Goose

"Bye-Bye, Baby Bunting" - Mother Goose

"One, Two, Buckle My Shoe" - Mother Goose (pages 20-21)
   Reproduce and cut apart rhyme (pages 20-21). Staple together to
   make individual books.

Songs:

"Baby Beluga" - Raffi in Baby Beluga (MCA)

Direct Instruction: /b/

1. Hold up a card with the letter Bb. Tell the children that it stands for
   the sound that they hear at the beginning of Bobby, Bruce and
   Bonnie. In isolating the sound (which really cannot be done) "clip it"
   with imaginary "scissors", inviting the children to do the same. Do not
   say "buh."

2. Ask the children to trace "Bb" on the carpet while making the sound it represents.

Working With Letters and Sounds

1. Ask children to draw three adjacent boxes called soundboxes on their chalkboards or papers.

2. Dictate the following words: <u>bottle</u>, <u>bath</u>, <u>rub</u>, <u>box</u>, <u>tub</u>, <u>basket</u>, <u>cub</u>, <u>bear</u>, <u>back</u>. Ask the children to indicate the position of the <u>b</u>.

b o x			c u b			b e a n		
b					b	b		

Direct Instruction: the

1. Show the children the word "the" within the context of a chart or big book. Tell them it is a very common word.

2. Let children walk around the room with clipboards, paper and pencil. Challenge them to see how many "the" words they can find. Every time they find one, they can write it down.

3. The sound of "th" could be introduced at this time, if children are familiar with many letter sounds.

Tip:
In order to prevent reversal problems, show the children that lower case "b" is inside capital "B."

Tip:
Make clipboards out of stiff cardboard and metal clips. Attach pencils with yarn.

Unit 1
Lesson 4

Activity for Home or School

On a card prepared by an adult, have the children trace over the word "the" with white glue. When the glue dries, the students can feel the letters.

Books to Enhance Comprehension, Skill and Language Development

Guided Reading:

The Farm - Andrea Butler (Rigby)

The Bath - Judy Nayer (Modern Curriculum Press, Ready Readers)

Independent Reading:

Add What Are You? - Andrea Butler (Rigby)

Writing Frame:

I am the _____.

Make Your Own Little Books:

Dress Up, pages 22-23. (Book 4)

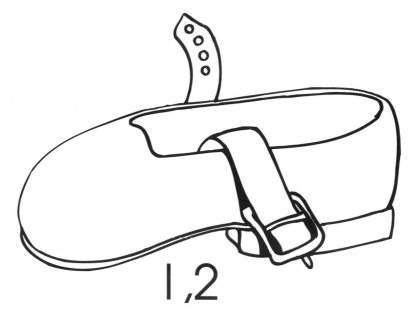

1,2
Buckle my shoe.

3,4
Shut the door.

5,6
Pick up sticks.

7,8
Don't be late!

9,10
A big
fat hen.

Reproducible

Words to Practice

I
am
the

Dress Up

Name _____

I am the monster.

I am the queen.

I am the king.

2

I am ME!

7

I am the bunny.

4

23
Reproducible

I am the pumpkin.

5

© Fearon Teacher Aids FE7948

Unit 1
Lesson 5

Sight Vocabulary:

- Review <u>I</u>, <u>the</u>
- Introduce <u>like</u>
- Phonics: /s/

Spelling: Sam, am, the, I

Grammar, Mechanics and Usage:
Capitalization of a person's name; writing a sentence

Developing Phonemic Awareness

Read Aloud:

<u>Green Eggs and Ham</u> - Dr. Seuss (Random House)

<u>Six Sleepy Sheep</u> - Jeffie Ross Gordon (Caroline House)

"Sing a Song of Six pence" - Mother Goose

"See Saw, Margery Daw" - Mother Goose

Shared Reading:

<u>Sing a Song</u> - June Melser (The Wright Group)

<u>School Bus</u> - Donald Crews (Scholastic, <u>Literacy Place</u> Big Book)

Songs:

"ABC Song" - Greg and Steve in <u>We All Live Together, Volume 1</u>
   (Youngheart Records)

"Sing a Song" - June Melser (Wright Group, Big Book)

Tip:

Make one continuous sound. Do not stop between sounds.

Direct Instruction: s

1. Point to the letter "s." Tell the children that it reminds you of a snake because it looks like one and it sounds like one: s-s-s-s. Let the children take turns hissing and crawling along the carpet in a snake-like manner.

2. Trace the "Ss" into the carpet while making its sound.

Blend, Read and Write

1. Review the sounds of "m" and "a."

2. Practice sound of "s."

24

Unit I Lesson 5

3. Blend and read:

Sam   sssăăămmm

4. Read and write: I am Sam.

Activity for Home or School
Give children clay or playdough. Let them roll it into snakes, S's and other letters.

Books to Enhance Reading Comprehension, Skill and Language Development

Guided Reading:
School Lunch - Polly Peterson (Modern Curriculum Press, Ready Readers)

The Circus - Andrea Butler (Rigby)

A Picnic in the Sand - Maryann Dobeck (Modern Curriculum Press, Ready Readers)

Independent Reading:
Add The Farm - Andrea Butler (Rigby)

Writing Frame:
I am _____.
I like _____.

Make Your Own Little Books:
Let children draw pictures of Sam from Green Eggs and Ham by Dr. Seuss (Random House). Put "I am Sam" in speech balloons. Bind papers together to make a book.

Sam, pages 26-27. (Book 5)

Tip:
Give lots of help. Let children work together. Children must feel successful.

Words to Practice

I
am
Sam
the

Sam

Name _____

8   1

✂ - ✂

Sam!   Sam!

6   3

Sam!

2

Here I am!

7

Sam!

4

Sam!

5

Unit 1
Lesson 6

Sight Vocabulary:

- **Review** I, the
- **Phonics:** ēe /ē/

Spelling: see, bee

Study Skill: locating color words on a chart

Grammar, Mechanics and Usage:
Period and question mark

Developing Phonemic Awareness

Read Aloud:

Sheep in a Jeep - Nancy Shaw (Houghton Mifflin)

Shared Reading:

Brown Bear, Brown Bear, What Do You See? - Bill Martin, Jr. (Holt)

Mary Wore Her Red Dress - Merle Peek (Houghton Mifflin, Literary Readers, Book A)

Eek! There's a Mouse in the House! - Wong Herbert Yee (Houghton Mifflin, Invitations to Literacy Big Book)

Direct Instruction: ēe

1. Tell the children that the sound they will learn today is easy because they already know it. Show the letter "Ee" and let the children tell you its name. Explain that the "Ee" often stands for that sound: ē. Write on the board and explain that the macron above the letter tells you that the ē stands for its long sound.

2. Say "cheese." Direct the students to look at the configuration of your mouth as you say this word. Let the children examine one another's mouths as they make the ē sound.

3. Write Ee on the board. Explain that two e's together usually represent the ē sound. Trace Ee onto the carpet while making the ē sound.

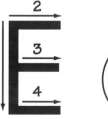

Tip:
Practice the capital "E" at a separate time.

Unit 1
Lesson 6

Blend, Read and Write

1. Review previously learned sounds and words.

2. Explain that two "e's" together usually represent the ē sound. Blend and read.

ēe   sēe   bēe

3. Write: I see the bee.

Activity for Home or School

Show the children how to find color words on a color chart.

Books to Enhance Reading Comprehension, Skill and Language Development

Guided Reading:

I See Colors - Creative Teaching Press

Independent Reading:

Add The Circus - Andrea Butler (Rigby)

Sing a Song - June Mesler (The Wright Group)

Writing Frame:

I see the [sticker or drawing] .

Make Your Own Little Books:

The Zoo, pages 30-31. (Book 6)

Letter Cards for Word Construction (page 300)

Word Cards for Sentence Construction (page 301)

Unit 1 Evaluation

Directions:

Ask each student to read the words and the sentence.

    the

    am

    I

    see

I see the bee.

Words to Practice

I
am
Sam
the
see
bee

The Zoo

Name _____

8

1

✂ - ✂

I see the giraffe.

6

I see the tiger.

3

I see the elephant.

2

I see the zoo.

7

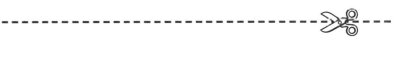

I see the snake.

4

I see the monkey.

5

31
Reproducible

Unit II

Target Word Recognition Skills:

/ŏ/, /c/, /t/, /n/, /d/, /f/, <u>a</u>, <u>is</u>

Unit II Lesson 1

Sight Vocabulary:

- Review <u>I</u>, <u>the</u>
- Introduce <u>color</u>
- Phonics: Hard "c" /k/

Spelling: I, the, red

Grammar, Mechanics and Usage: Sentence and period

Developing Phonemic Awareness

Read Aloud:

<u>The Carrot Seed</u> - Ruth Kraus (Harper & Row)

<u>Corduroy</u> - Don Freeman (Puffin)

<u>Color Dance</u> - Ann Jonas (Greenwillow)

<u>A Color of His Own</u> - Leo Lionni (Pantheon)

<u>Freight Train</u> - Donald Crews (Greenwillow)

Shared Reading:

<u>Mary Wore Her Red Dress</u> - Merle Peek (Clarion) also in <u>Beginning to Read, Book A</u> (Houghton Mifflin, <u>Literary Readers</u>)

<u>The Very Hungry Caterpillar</u> - Eric Carle (Houghton Mifflin, <u>Invitations to Reading</u> Big Book)

Rhymes and Poems:

"Orange Is a Carrot" - Marlene & Robert McCracken

"Who Took the Cookies from the Cookie Jar?" - Traditional

    Who took the cookies from the cookie jar?

    <u>[Child's name]</u> took the cookies from the cookie jar.

    Who, me?

    Yes, you.

    Couldn't be.

    Then who?

    <u>[Another child's name]</u> took the cookies from the cookie jar.

Song:

"ABC Song" - Greg and Steve in <u>We All Live Together, Volume 1</u> (Youngheart Records)

Unit II
Lesson 1

Direct Instruction: Hard "c" /k/

1. Show the children the letter Cc. Explain that this letter stands for two sounds. The sound they will learn today is the /k/ sound, the sound at the beginning of cat, Carrie, and Curt. Invite the children to make the sound as they "write" the Cc on their desktops or carpet, using the index and middle fingers.

2. Hold up a sack in which you have some hard candy. Tell the children to try to guess what is in your sack. Give them one clue: the hidden objects begin with the /k/ sound. When someone guesses "candy" take it out and tell the students that it is hard candy. We call the /k/ sound of c "hard."

3. Pass out one piece of candy to every child who can give you a word that begins with hard c. Of course, everyone will eventually "win."

Working With Letters and Sounds

1. Ask the children to draw three adjacent squares called soundboxes on their chalkboards or papers.

2. Dictate the following words: cat, call, pick, came, sick, stick, come, care. Ask the students to indicate the position of the /k/ sound by writing "c" in the first or last box.

come

lick

Blend, Read and Write

1. Review previously learned sounds.

2. Write: I see the cab.

Unit II
Lesson 1

Activity for Home or School

1. Prepare one sentence strip for each child.

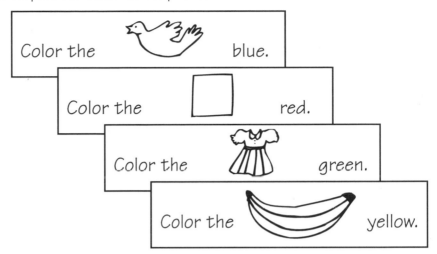

2. Read each strip, showing the class how you refer to the color chart to identify the color word.

3. After reading each strip, pass them out to the children to color.

Books to Enhance Reading Comprehension, Skill and Language Development

Guided Reading:

The Cat Came Back - Carly Easton (Modern Curriculum Press, Ready Readers)

A Toy Box (Rigby)

Independent Reading:

Add color word books

Writing Frame:

I see the red [sticker, picture or phonetic spelling] .

Make Your Own Little Books:

Color, pages 37-38. (Book 7)

Letter Cards for Word Construction (page 302)

Word Cards for Sentence Construction (page 303)

Color Word Flashcards (page 36)

Copy cards on white paper. Cut them out and color the backs with the appropriate colors. Encourage children to take the cards home to practice.

Color Word Flashcards

Cut out the cards. Color the back with the appropriate color. Take the cards home to practice.

blue

yellow

orange

black

red

green

purple

brown

36

Reproducible

Words to Practice

color
the

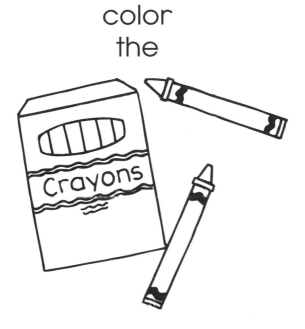

8

Color

Name _____

1

Color the house.

6

Color the bird.

3

37
Reproducible

Color the tree.

2

Color the rainbow.

7

Color the sun.

4

Color the flowers.

5

38
Reproducible

© Fearon Teacher Aids FE7948

Unit II
Lesson 2

Sight Vocabulary: is

- **Phonics: /t/**

Spelling: at, cat, bat, mat, sat, is

Grammar, Mechanics and Usage:
Starting a sentence with a capital letter; ending with a period or question mark.

Developing Phonemic Awareness

Read Aloud:
Is It Red? Is It Yellow? Is It Blue? - Tana Hoban (Greenwillow)
"Little Tommy Tucker" - Mother Goose
"Hickory Dickory Dock" - Mother Goose

Shared Reading:
When This Box Is Full - Patricia Lillie (Houghton Mifflin, Invitations to
    Literacy Big Book)
"Orange Is a Carrot" Marlene and Robert McCracken
To Town - Joy Cowley (Wright Group)

Direct Instruction: /t/

1. Ask the children to listen carefully. Can they hear a clock ticking? (Make the t - t - t sound yourself, without moving your lips).

2. Tell the children that this is the sound represented by the letter Tt (show letter). Wave your arm like a pendulum, inviting the children to join you, while making the t sound.

3. Trace the lower case t into the carpet, desk, or air while making the t sound.

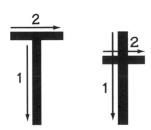

Unit II
Lesson 2

Tip:
Guide (model) writing activity until children are sure of proper letter formation.

Tip:
Have the children write the letters themselves on blank squares. This is good handwriting practice.

Working With Letters and Sounds

1. Ask children to draw three adjacent squares called *soundboxes* on their chalkboards or papers.

2. Dictate the following words: <u>c</u>at, <u>t</u>able, <u>t</u>eacher, <u>t</u>at, <u>t</u>at, <u>t</u>ool, <u>t</u>ime, <u>c</u>ut. Ask children to write <u>t</u> in the beginning or ending position.

Blend, Read and Write

1. Review previously learned sounds.

2. Practice sound represented by "t." Make quick staccato sounds. Do not say "tuh."

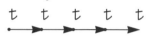

3. Blend and read:

4. Read and Write: I see the cat.

Word Construction

1. Ask the children to sort for the following letters (page 304):

| s | t | c | b | a | m | e | e |

2. Ask children to make the following words: <u>cat</u>, <u>sat</u>, <u>mat</u>, <u>see</u>, <u>bee</u>, <u>cab</u>, <u>am</u>, <u>at</u>.

Direct Instruction: is

1. Read the poem "Orange Is A Carrot," (Marlene and Robert McCracken). Print the poem on a chart.

2. Frame the word "is" for the children. Ask the children to find other places where the word occurs.

3. Give each child a card on which the word <u>is</u> has been printed. Let the children trace over the word with crayon or white glue. Make sure they add <u>is</u> to their sight word collection.

Unit II
Lesson 2

Books to Enhance Reading Comprehension, Skill and Language Development

Guided Reading:

The Hat - Alex Starr (Modern Curriculum Press, Ready Readers)

Toot Toot - Brian Wildsmith (Oxford University Press)

Teeny Tiny Tina - (Rigby)

Jack-in-the-Box - (Rigby)

Two Turtles - Carly Easton (Modern Curriculum Press, Ready Readers)

Independent Reading:

Add I See Colors (Creative Teaching Press)

A Toy Box (Rigby)

Activity for Home or School

Copy the sentence strips (below) on white paper. Divide an 8½" x 11" (21.3cm x 27.5cm) sheet of paper into fourths. Cut out and glue one strip in each section. Have children illustrate the sentences.

Writing Frame:

The cat is _____.

Make Your Own Little Books:

Toys, pages 42-43. (Book 8)

Letter Cards for Word Construction (page 304)

Word Cards for Sentence Construction (page 305)

The bat is black.

The bee is yellow.

The mat is red.

The cat is orange.

Words to Practice

I
the
see
at
cat
mat
sat

8

Toys

Name _____

1

✂ - ✂

I see the brown bear.

6

I see the yellow bat.

3

I see the orange cat.

2

I see the toys.

7

I see the red bicycle.

4

I see the blue doll.

5

43
Reproducible

Unit II
Lesson 3

Sight Vocabulary:

- Review I, the, is
- Introduce no
- Phonics and Structural Analysis: /n/; contraction "can't"

Spelling: an, can, man, tan, no

Grammar, Mechanics and Usage:
The apostrophe, capitalization of a person's name.

Developing Phonemic Awareness

Read Aloud:

The Napping House - Audry Wood (Harcourt)

Noisy Nora - Rosemary Wells (Dial)

There's a Nightmare in My Closet - Mercer Mayer (Dial)

Shared Reading:

Oh, No! - (Rigby, Big Book)

Rhymes and Poems:

"I Had a Little Nut Tree" - Mother Goose

No Jumping on the Bed - Tedd Arnold (Dial)

Song:

"If You're Happy and You Know It" - Greg and Steve in We All Live
Together, Volume III (Youngheart Records)

Direct Instruction: /n/

1. Show the children the word No. Involve them in this cheerleader type chant:

Teacher:	Boys and girls, how do you spell no?
Children:	N - O
Teacher:	(louder) How do you spell No?
Children:	N - O
Teacher:	Give me an "N."
Children:	"N."
Teacher:	Give me an "O."
Children:	"O."
Teacher:	N - O spells . . .
Children:	NO!

Unit II Lesson 3

2. Congratulate the children on knowing how to spell the word <u>no</u>. Tell them that you can tell they also know the sound of the letter "n," the sound that they hear at the beginning of <u>Nicky</u>, <u>Natalie</u>, and <u>Nelly</u>. Demonstrate how you must position your tongue as you make the "n" sound. Let the children try it.

3. Trace the lower case "n" into the carpet, desk, or air as you make the "n" sound.

Working With Letters and Sounds

1. Ask children to draw three adjacent squares called soundboxes on their chalkboards or papers.

2. Dictate the following words: <u>number</u>, <u>nice</u>, <u>can</u>, <u>fallen</u>, <u>ran</u>, <u>note</u>, <u>run</u>, <u>nut</u>.

3. Ask the children to indicate the position of the <u>n</u> sound by writing "n" in the first or last box.

Blend, Read and Write

1. Review previously learned sounds.

2. Practice the sound of <u>n</u>.

    n

3. Blend and read:

| an | can | can't |
| man | Nan | tan |

4. Read and write: Nan can see the cat.

Word Construction

1. Distribute the following letter cards (page 306) to each child:

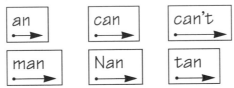

2. Ask the children to make the following words: <u>can</u>, <u>an</u>, <u>at</u>, <u>Nan</u>, <u>ban</u>, <u>man</u>, <u>mat</u>, <u>sat</u>, <u>beet</u>. Other possible words: <u>no</u>, <u>can't</u>, <u>cat</u>, <u>see</u>, <u>bee</u>.

Unit II Lesson 3

Learning With Language Experience

1. Ask the children what they can do. Record their responses on chart paper.

> I can ride. — Raul
>
> I can dress myself. — Barbie
>
> I can tie my shoes. — Joseph

2. Prepare sentence strips (or cut up the chart). Ask the children to copy their sentences onto large sheets of paper and draw pictures to illustrate them. Bind the pages together to make an "I Can" book.

Books to Enhance Reading Comprehension, Skill and Language Development

Guided Reading:

I Can Read - (Creative Teaching Press)

Socks - Mary Solins (Modern Curriculum Press, Ready Readers)

Independent Reading:

Add Toot Toot - Brian Wildsmith (Oxford University Press)

Teeny Tiny Tina - (Rigby)

Jack-in-the Box - (Rigby)

Writing Frame:

I can_____.

I can_____.

I can_____.

but I can't _____.

Make Your Own Little Books:

Finding Cats, pages 47-48. (Book 9)

Letter Cards for Word Construction (page 306)

Word Cards for Sentence Construction (page 307)

Words to Practice

I
the
see
an
can
man
Nan
tan

8

Finding Cats

Name _____

1

I can see the brown cat.

6

I see the orange cat.

3

47
Reproducible

© Fearon Teacher Aids FE7948

I can see the black cat.

2

I can't see the black and white cat!

7

I can see the white cat.

4

I can see the gray cat.

5

Unit II Lesson 4

Sight Vocabulary:

- Review <u>the</u>, <u>I</u>, <u>is</u>, <u>color</u>, <u>no</u>
- Introduce <u>a</u> (I see <u>a</u> cat.)
- Phonics: /ō/

Spelling: on, Mom, Tom, cot, not

Grammar, Mechanics and Usage:
Capital letter for a person's name

Developing Phonemic Awareness

Read Aloud:

<u>Hop on Pop</u> - Dr. Seuss (Random House)

<u>Ten Black Dots</u> - Donald Crews (Scribner)

"Higglety, Pigglety, Pop" - Mother Goose

"Hot Cross Buns" - Mother Goose

"Tom, Tom, the Piper's Son" - Mother Goose

Shared Reading:

<u>When This Box Is Full</u>   Patricia Lillie (Houghton Mifflin, <u>Invitations to Literacy</u>, Big Book)

<u>The Little Red Hen</u> - Retold by Brenda Parkes (Rigby, Big Book)

<u>On Top of Spaghetti</u> - Katherine Tillotson (Houghton Mifflin, <u>Invitations to Literacy</u>, Big Book)

Rhymes and Poems:

<u>Gobble Gobble Glup Glup</u> (Rigby, Big Book)

<u>Time for Rhyme</u> (Rigby)

Song:

"My Dog's Bigger Than Your Dog"

    My dog's bigger than your dog

    My dog's bigger than yours.

    My dog's bigger 'cause he eats _____.

    My dog's bigger than yours.

        —Old Kennel Ration Advertisement

Unit II
Lesson 4

Direct Instruction: /ŏ/

1. Tell the children that they will learn one sound represented by the letter "o." (Show letter) Explain that this sound is very easy to remember because it is the sound you make when the doctor says "Say ŏ." Then you open your mouth like an "o" and you say " ŏ."

2. Explain that the breve above the letter (ŏ) tells us that the "o" says its short name.

3. Trace the "o" into the carpet while making its short sound.

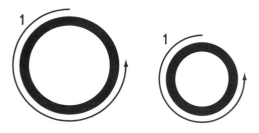

Blend, Read and Write

1. Practice previously learned sounds.

2. Practice the sound represented by "o."

3. Blend and read:

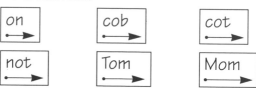

on   cob   cot

not   Tom   Mom

Word Construction

1. Have the children sort for the following letters (page 308):

ŏ   T   c   b   n   s   m   M   e   e   t

2. Make these words: on, not, cot, cob, sob, see, Mom, Tom.

50

Unit II
Lesson 4

Books to Enhance Reading Comprehension, Skill and Language Development

Guided Reading:
Cat on the Mat - Brian Wildsmith (Oxford University Press)
Stop! - Eric Rose (Modern Curriculum Press, Ready Readers)

Independent Reading:
Add I Can Read - (Creative Teaching Press)

Innovation on Text

1. Show the children how they can change the text of the book Cat on the Mat - Brian Wildsmith (Oxford University Press).

   For example:
   The bear sat on the mat.

2. Help the children compose their own sentences. Take their dictation. Illustrate and bind the pages together to make new books.

Writing Frame:
I can see a _____.

Make Your Own Little Books:

1. Tom, pages 52-53. (Book 10)

2. Say "I can see Juan. Who can you see?" Encourage the pattern "I can see _____. Write down the responses and ask children to illustrate. Bind the pages into a book.

I can see Juan.

I can see Marilu.

Letter Cards for Word Construction (page 308)

Word Cards for Sentence Construction (page 309)

51

Words to Practice

see	cot
a	not
can	Mom
	Tom
	cob
	sob

Tom

Name _____

Tom can not see Mom!

Tom can see a truck.

Tom can see a ball.

2

"Wa-a-ah!"

7

✂- ✂

Tom can see a
baseball bat.

4

Tom can see
a bike.

5

53
Reproducible

Unit II
Lesson 5

Sight Vocabulary:

- Review <u>I</u>, <u>is</u>, <u>the</u>, <u>a</u>, <u>no</u>, <u>color</u>
- Phonics: /d/

Spelling: bad, mad, sad, and, band, sand

Grammar, Mechanics and Usage:
Word order, the apostrophe, indefinite articles <u>a</u>, <u>an</u>

Structural Analysis: Contractions

Developing Phonemic Awareness

Read Aloud:

<u>Make Way for the Ducklings</u> - Robert McCloskey (Viking)

<u>There's An Ant in Anthony</u> - Bernard Most (Mulberry)

<u>Ten Black Dots</u> - Donald Crews (Greenwillow)

Shared Reading:

<u>The Chick and the Duckling</u> - Mira Ginsburg (Macmillan)

<u>Have You Seen My Duckling?</u> - Nancy Tafuri (Greenwillow)

<u>All Fall Down</u> - Brian Wildsmith (Oxford University Press)

Rhymes and Poems:

"Diddle Diddle Dumpling" - Mother Goose

"Ding, Dong, Dell" - Mother Goose

"A Dillar, A Dollar" - Mother Goose

Songs:

"Five Little Ducks" - Raffi in <u>Rise and Shine</u> (Troubadour Records, Ltd.)

<u>The Farmer in the Dell</u> - (Publications International Limited)

Direct Instruction: /d/

1. Show the children the lower case <u>d</u>. Tell them it reminds you of a doorknob and a door. Draw a picture to illustrate.

"doorknob"

"door"

Unit II
Lesson 5

2. Teach the children to say:

> First you make the doorknob
> Then the door - d - d - d .

3. Have the children trace lower case "d" while reciting the rhyme and the sound.

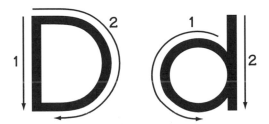

Working With Letters and Sounds

1. Ask children to draw three adjacent squares called soundboxes on their chalkboards or papers.

2. Dictate the following words, while the children write the "d" in the first or last box: <u>donut</u>, <u>had</u>, <u>need</u>, <u>dig</u>, <u>don't</u>, <u>feed</u>, <u>dozen</u>, <u>bed</u>.

Blend, Read, and Write

1. Review previously learned sounds.

2. Practice the sound represented by "d." Make quick, staccato-like sounds.

d   d   d
•   •   • →

3. Blend and read:

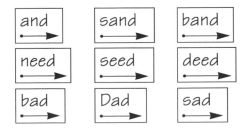

and →	sand →	band →
need →	seed →	deed →
bad →	Dad →	sad →

4. Read and write: Dad is not sad.

Unit II Lesson 5

Word Construction

1. Ask the children to sort for the following letters (page 310).

| a | b | c | d | m | n | o | s | e | e | t | D | N | m |

2. Make some of the following words: need, seed, Dad, sad, bad, mad, seen, beet, and, band, sand, Mom, at, bat, cat, mat, Nat, an, Dan, can, tan, man, see, bee.

Activity for Home or School: Sentence Making

Reproduce the worksheet on page 57. Ask the children to cut out the words and make as many sentences as they can. Teach the use of the words a, and an.

Books to Enhance Reading Comprehension, Skill and Language Development

Guided Reading:

All Fall Down - Brian Wildsmith (Oxford University Press)

Story Time - Polly Peterson (Modern Curriculum Press, Ready Readers)

Independent Reading:

Add Cat on the Mat - Brian Wildsmith (Oxford University Press)

Make Your Own Little Books

Ann and Dan, pages 58-59. (Book 11)

Letter Cards for Word Construction (page 310)

Word Cards for Sentence Construction (page 311)

I	see
ant	mat
an	the
is	bee
The	need
a	seed
cat	black
bat	yellow

Reproducible

Words to Practice

a	and
can't	band
can	sand

Ann and Dan

Name _____

8

1

- -

Ann and Dan can
read, but. . .

6

Ann and Dan can swim.

3

Ann and Dan can jump.

2

Ann and Dan can't skate.

7

Ann and Dan
can play ball.

4

Ann and Dan
can dance.

5

© Fearon Teacher Aids FE7948

Unit II
Lesson 6

Sight Vocabulary:

- Review <u>the</u>, <u>is</u>, <u>a</u>, <u>I</u>, <u>color</u>, <u>no</u>
- Phonics: /f/

Spelling: fat, fan, feed, feet

Grammar, Mechanics and Usage: Adding "s" (needs)

Developing Phonemic Awareness

Read Aloud:

<u>Freight Train</u> - Donald Crews (Greenwillow)

<u>Fish Eyes</u> - Lois Ehlert (Harcourt Brace)

<u>Fish Is Fish</u> - Leo Lionni (Pantheon)

<u>Faint Frogs Feeling Feverish and Other Terrific Tongue Twisters</u> - Lilian Obligado

Shared Reading:

<u>Fishy Facts</u> - Ivan Chermayeff (Houghton Mifflin, <u>Invitations to Literacy</u>, Big Book)

<u>Jack and the Beanstalk</u> - Judith Smith (Rigby, Big Book)

<u>Cat Goes Fiddle-I-Fee</u> - Paul Galdone (Houghton Mifflin, <u>Literary Readers, Book B</u>)

Rhymes and Poem:

"Fish" - Jack Prelutsky in <u>Poems to Read to the Very Young</u> (Random House)

"A New Friend" - Marjorie Allen Anderson in <u>Poems to Read to the Very Young</u> (Random House)

Song:

"Fee - Fie - Foe - Fum" (Wright Group, Big Book and Tape)

Direct Instruction: /f/

1. Show children a package of fish-shaped crackers. Hold up the letter <u>Ff</u> and tell students that it represents the sound they hear at the beginning of <u>fish</u>: /f/ /f/ /f/.

2. Have the children trace the lower case <u>f</u> into the carpet as they make its sound.

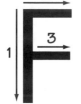

Unit II
Lesson 6

3. Ask children for other words that begin with "f." Give crackers for correct responses.

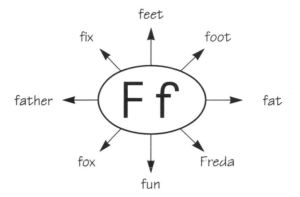

Working With Letters and Sounds

1. Ask children to make three adjacent squares called soundboxes on their chalkboards or papers.

2. Dictate the following words: <u>fat</u>, <u>feet</u>, <u>stiff</u>, fast, fix, knife, life, <u>follow</u>, <u>first</u>, <u>wife</u>.

3. Ask children to write the "f" in the first or last box.

Blend, Read and Write

1. Review previously learned sounds.

2. Practice the sound represented by "f."

f

3. Blend and read:

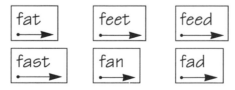

| fat | feet | feed |
| fast | fan | fad |

4. Read and write: The man needs a fan.

Unit II
Lesson 6

Books to Enhance Reading Comprehension, Skill and Language Development

Guided Reading:

<u>Fruit Salad</u> - (Rigby)

<u>Time for Lunch</u> - Kathryn E. Lewis (Modern Curriculum Press, <u>Ready Readers</u>)

Independent Reading:

<u>All Fall Down</u> - Brian Wildsmith (Oxford University Press)

Add <u>Cat on the Mat</u> - Brian Wildsmith (Oxford University Press)

Make Your Own Little Books:

1. <u>The Couch</u>, pages 63-64. (Book 12)

2. Ask the children what they can do. Encourage the response "I can . . ." Record their responses on large sheets of paper. Illustrate and bind the pages together to make a decodable book.

"I can run,"
said Antonio.

"I can read,"
said Alonso.

"I can dance,"
said Karina.

"I can go to the
park," said Joey

Or copy each child's work (must be in black marker) and make a book for each child.

Letter Cards for Word Construction (page 312)

Word Cards for Sentence Construction (page 313)

Unit II Evaluation

Directions:

Ask each child to read the lists of words and the sentence. Ask the child to write:

I can see a cat.
I can not see the man.

List A	List B
the	at
a	can
is	not
I	am
on	

Words to Practice

the   at
on   bat
              cat
              fat
              mat
              sat

The Couch

Name _____

8

1

The fat cat sat
on the couch.

6

Mom sat on the couch.

3

Reproducible

Dad sat on the couch.

2

Uh-oh!

7

Pam sat on the couch.

4

Sam sat on the couch.

5

Unit III

Target Word
Recognition
Skills:

/p/, /r/, /h/, /l/, /g/, /ĭ/,
<u>said</u>, <u>of</u>, <u>to</u>, <u>go</u>, <u>as</u>, <u>if</u>

Sight Vocabulary:

- Introduce: <u>said</u>
- Phonics and Structural Analysis: /p/ I'm

Spelling: said, I'm

Grammar, Mechanics and Usage:

Comma, quotation marks, apostrophe

Developing Phonemic Awareness

Read Aloud:

<u>Each Peach Pear Plum</u> - Janet and Allen Ahlberg (Viking)

<u>Pig Pig Grows Up</u> - David McPhail (Houghton Mifflin)

<u>The Princess and the Pea</u> - Hans Christian Andersen (North-South
 Books)

<u>A Pocket for Corduroy</u> - Don Freeman (Puffin)

Shared Reading:

<u>The Three Little Pigs</u> - Brenda Parkes (Rigby, Big Book)

<u>Pumpkin, Pumpkin</u> - Jean Titherington (Houghton Mifflin, <u>Invitations to
 Literacy</u>, Big Book)

Rhymes and Poems:

"Polly, Put the Kettle On" - Mother Goose

"Pease Porridge Hot" - Mother Goose

"Peter Piper" - Mother Goose

"Peter, Peter, Pumpkin Eater" - Mother Goose

Songs:

"I'm a Little Teapot" - <u>Singing Bee</u> (Lothrop, Lee and Shephard)

Goober Peas - (Wright Group, Big Book and Tape)

Direct Instruction: /p/

1. Show the children the letter "Pp." Tell them that the sound it
 represents makes you think of "exploding air." Ask them if they can
 guess why as you recite the following tongue twister:

    Peter Piper picked a peck of pickled peppers.

2. Hold the palm of your hand in front of your mouth as you recite the
 twister. Ask children to join in several times. Make sure they hold the
 palms of their hands close to their mouths so they can feel the air

**Unit III
Lesson 1**

3. Trace the lower case "p" on the carpet while making the "p" sound.

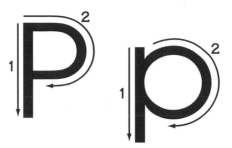

4. Brainstorm words that begin with "p."

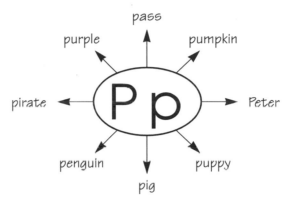

pass

purple   pumpkin

pirate   Pp   Peter

penguin   puppy

pig

Working With Letters and Sounds

1. Ask the children to draw three adjacent squares called soundboxes on their chalkboards or papers.

2. Dictate the following words: <u>pot</u>, <u>lip</u>, <u>cup</u>, <u>pearl</u>, <u>pig</u>, <u>lap</u>, <u>present</u>, <u>paper</u>. Ask the children to indicate the position of the "p" sound by writing lower case "p" in the first or last box.

pig   lap

Blend, Read and Write

1. Blend and read:

păt   pŏt   păn   căp   tăp   pĕep

2. Read and write: The pot is not hot.

Unit III
Lesson 1

Word Construction

1. Ask the children to sort for the following letters (page 314):

| p | ŏ | ă | t | n | s | f |

2. Make the following words: pot, pat, pan, past, fat, nap, tap, top

Direct Instruction: I'm, said

1. Sing "I'm a Little Teapot" while pointing to the words on a chart.

2. Explain that "I'm" is another contraction, or short way of writing "I am." Review (reteach) the word "apostrophe." Explain that this mark tells us a letter or letters have been left out of two words to make a shorter word.

3. Say "I'm a teacher (person, etc.). What are you?"

   Record the children's responses on a chart, introducing the students to the quotation marks, the word said and the comma before said.

   "I'm a boy," said Chris.
   "I'm a ballerina," said Reva.

4. Rewrite the sentences (or cut up the chart). Ask the children to illustrate their dictated sentences. Bind the pages into a book. Have the children choose a suitable title.

Books to Enhance Reading Comprehension, Skill and Language Development

Guided Reading:
Pink Pig - Tim Anton (Modern Curriculum Press, Ready Readers)
Who's Coming for a Ride? (Rigby)

Independent Reading:
Add Fruit Salad (Rigby)
All Fall Down - Brian Wildsmith (Oxford University Press)

Make Your Own Little Books
What Are You? pages 69-70. (Book 13)

Letter Cards for Word Construction (page 314)

Word Cards for Sentence Construction (page 315)

Words to Practice

I'm   at
said   bat
             cat
             fat
             mat
             pat
             sat

8

What Are You?

Name _____

1

"I'm a pilot,"
said Nan.

6

"I'm a pirate,"
said Tom.

3

"I'm a policeman."
said Pat.

2

"I'm a dad,"
said Dad.

7

"I'm a pumpkin,"
said Ann.

4

"I'm a pig,"
said Matt.

5

Unit III
Lesson 2

Sight Vocabulary:

- Review <u>said,</u> <u>like</u>
- Introduce <u>to</u>
- Phonics and Structural Analysis: /l/

Spelling: like, to

Grammar, Mechanics and Usage:
Review punctuation for a simple sentence. Introduce possessive ('s).

Developing Phonemic Awareness

Read Aloud:

<u>Leo the Late Bloomer</u> - Robert Kraus (Scholastic, <u>Literacy Place</u>)

<u>Look</u> - Michael Grejniec (North-South Books)

<u>I Like to Be Little</u> - Charlotte Zolotow (Thomas Crowell)

<u>I Like Books</u> - Anthony Browne (Knopf)

Shared Reading:

<u>Lazy Mary</u> - Jane Melser (Wright Group, Big Book)

<u>To Market To Market</u> - (Wright Group, Big Book)

Rhymes and Poems:

"I Like Bugs" - Margaret Wise Brown in <u>The Fish With the Deep Blue Smile</u> (Dutton) p. 74

"Little Miss Muffet" - Mother Goose

"Little Boy Blue" - Mother Goose

"Little Jack Horner" - Mother Goose

"Lucy Locket" - Mother Goose

"Ladybird, Ladybird" - Mother Goose

Songs:

"I Love the Mountains" - Nellie Edge Big Book and Tape

"Love Somebody" (See page 2.)

"Loop 'D Loo" - Greg and Steve in <u>We All Live Together, Volume I</u> (Youngheart Records)

Direct Instruction: /l/

1. Show the children the letter "Ll." Tell them this is a very special letter because it is the first letter of the word "love." Sing (make up a tune) or recite the following jingle.

L-O-V-E, love
L-O-V-E, love
I love you
You love me
L-O-V-E, love.

Ask the children to join you.

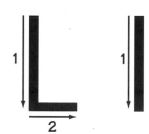

2. Trace the lower case "l" onto the carpet while making the "l" sound.

3. Brainstorm "Ll" words.

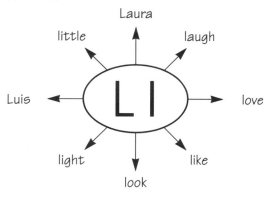

Working With Letters and Sounds

1. Ask the children to draw three adjacent squares called *soundboxes* on their chalkboards or papers.

2. Dictate the following words: <u>like</u>, <u>fill</u>, <u>lot</u>, <u>listen</u>, <u>leg</u>, <u>will</u>, <u>all</u>, <u>love</u>. Ask the children to indicate the position of the "l" sound by writing "l" in the first or last box.

Blend, Read, and Write

1. Blend and read:

2. Read and write: Bob lost the cap.

Unit III
Lesson 2

Word Construction

1. Ask the children to sort for the following letters (page 316):

| l | ă | p | d | t | ŏ | m | n | s |

2. Make the following words: <u>land</u>, <u>lot</u>, <u>lap</u>, <u>last</u>, <u>lost</u>.

Direct Instruction: <u>to</u>

1. Tell the children about something you like to do (I like to travel). Write it for them, emphasizing the word <u>to</u>.

> I like to run.
> — Jose

2. Ask them to tell you what they like to do. As each child responds, write her answer on a large sheet of paper. When you get to the word <u>to</u>, say "Help me spell <u>to</u>."

3. Ask each child to illustrate her sentence. Bind the pages together to make a book. Ask the children to choose a suitable title.

4. Ask the students to write <u>to</u> on an index card. Have them trace the word with white glue or crayon. Assign for homework and remind children to add the word to their word collection.

Books to Enhance Reading Comprehension, Skill and Language Development

Guided Reading:
<u>Just Like Daddy</u> - Frank Asch (Houghton Mifflin, <u>Literacy Readers, Book B</u>)

<u>Look Closer</u> - Claudia Logan (Modern Curriculum Press, <u>Ready Readers</u>)

Independent Reading:
Add <u>Who's Coming for a Ride?</u> - (Rigby)

Writing Frame:
I like to _____.
I like to _____.
I like to _____.
but I don't like to _____.

Make Your Own Little Books:
<u>I Like</u>, pages 74-75. (Book 14)

Letter Cards for Word Construction (page 316)

Word Cards for Sentence Construction (page 317)

Tip:
Do this orally first, using pocket chart.

Words to Practice

I

like

to

"I Like"

Name _____

8

1

 -

I like to paint.

6

I like to skate.

3

I like to ride my bike.

2

I like to play ball.

7

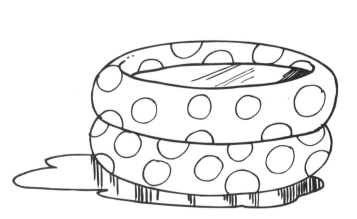

I like to swim.

4

I like to read.

5

Unit III
Lesson 3

Sight Vocabulary:

■ Review <u>said</u>, <u>to</u>
■ Introduce <u>of</u>
■ Phonics and Structural Analysis: /r/, -an, can, Dan, fan, man, ran, tan

Spelling: of, an, can, fan, man, tan

Grammar, Mechanics and Usage:

The comma to represent a pause in a sentence

Developing Phonemic Awareness

Read Aloud:

<u>Little Red Riding Hood</u> - Trina S. Hyman (Houghton Mifflin)

<u>The Red Racer</u> - Audrey Wood (Simon & Schuster)

Shared Reading:

<u>It Begins with A</u> - Stephanie Calmenson (Scholastic, <u>Literacy Place</u>, Big Book)

<u>The Gingerbread Man</u> - Brenda Parkes (Rigby Big Book)

<u>Rosie's Walk</u> - Pat Hutchins (Macmillan, Big Book)

Rhymes:

"Rain Rain, Go Away" - Mother Goose

"Ring Around the Rosie" - Mother Goose

"Roses Are Red" - Mother Goose

Songs:

"Row, Row, Row Your Boat" - Raffi in <u>Rise and Shine</u> (Troubadour Records Ltd.)

"Roll Over" - Merle Peek (Houghton Mifflin)

Direct Instruction: /r/

1. Let the children pretend to get inside cars (you might want to push chairs together). Rev up the "engines" with the "r" sound: r-r-r-r. Tell the children that this is the sound represented by the letter "Rr."

2. Have the children trace the lower case "r" onto the carpet as they "rev" up their engines: r-r-r-r-r.

Working With Letters and Sounds

1. Ask the children to draw three adjacent squares called soundboxes on their chalkboards or papers.

2. Dictate the following words: <u>run</u>, <u>rabbit</u>, <u>deer</u>, <u>hear</u>, <u>fur</u>, <u>race</u>, <u>wear</u>, <u>right</u>, <u>ring</u>, <u>bear</u>. Ask the children to indicate the position of the "r" sound by writing the letter in the first or last box.

run   bear

Blend, Read and Write

1. Blend and read:

| rat | ran | rob | deer | rot |

| Ron | rap |

2. Write: Ron and Ann ran fast.

Word Construction

1. Ask the children to sort for following letters (page 318):

r ă t ŏ d b e e n

2. Make the following words: <u>rat</u>, <u>reed</u>, <u>deer</u>, <u>rod</u>, <u>ran</u>, <u>rot</u>, <u>rob</u>.

Direct Instruction: of

1. Read "Sing a Song of Sixpence" or another rhyme that has the word "of" in it. Track the words on a chart or Big Book. Frame the word <u>of</u> and explain that this is a word that is pronounced "uv" even though it is spelled "o-f."

Unit III
Lesson 3

2. Give the children the opportunity to look through books and charts to find other places where the word <u>of</u> is used. Challenge the students to copy the word on their clipboards every time they find it.

3. Write "of" on index cards. Trace with crayon or glue. Practice at home.

Activity for Home or School: of

1. Hide various objects (toys, candy, etc.) around the room. Prepare sentence strips that describe the location of the hidden item.

> A red candy is on top of the blue box.

2. Let the children try to locate the hidden "surprise" by reading the strip. Model these word recognition strategies:

   1. Start again.
   2. Read to the end of the sentence. Skip unknown word or words.
   3. Look at the first letter of the unknown word. Make its sound.
   4. Look at the other letters. Blend the sounds.
   5. Does your word make sense?
   6. Try again.

Books to Enhance Reading Comprehension, Skill and Language Development

Guided Reading:

<u>Red or Blue</u> - Jenni Stevens (Modern Curriculum Press, <u>Ready Readers</u>)

<u>The Birthday Cake</u> - (Rigby)

Independent Reading:

Add <u>Just Like Daddy</u> - Frank Asch (Houghton Mifflin, <u>Literacy Readers, Book B</u>)

Make Your Own Little Books:

<u>The Gingerbread Man</u>, pages 79-80. (Book 15)

Letter Cards for Word Construction (page 318)

Word Cards for Sentence Construction (page 319)

Words to Practice

away	an
after	can
him	Dan
got	fan
	man
	pan
	tan

The gingerbread man
ran away.

2

The fox got him.

7

The woman ran
after him.

4

The boy ran
after him.

5

80
Reproducible

Unit III
Lesson 4

Sight Vocabulary:

- Review <u>said</u>, <u>to</u>, <u>of</u>
- Introduce <u>if</u>
- Phonics and Structural Analysis: /ĭ/; inflectional ending "_ed" (looked); phonogram "_it" (bit, sit, etc.).

Spelling: it, bit, fit, lit, pit, sit, if, in

Grammar, Mechanics and Usage:
Review conventions already introduced.

Developing Phonemic Awareness

Read Aloud:

<u>Inch By Inch</u> - Leo Lionni (Scholastic)

<u>Swimmy</u> - Leo Lionni (Scholastic)

Shared Reading:

<u>It Looked Like Spilt Milk</u> - Charles Shaw (Harper & Row, Big Book)

<u>The Itsy Bitsy Spider</u> - Iza Trapani (Houghton Mifflin, <u>Invitations to Literacy</u>, Big Book)

Rhyme:

"The Pickety Fence" - David McCord in <u>Everytime I Climb a Tree</u> (Little Brown)

Song:

"If You're Happy and You Know It" - Greg and Steve in <u>We All Live Together, Volume III</u> (Youngheart Records)

Tip:

Short <u>i</u> is very difficult for children. Tell a silly story or use a mnemonic motion, such as "dotting" (touching) your nose every time you make that sound.

Direct Instruction: /ĭ/

1. Tell the students that the short "i" sound reminds you of a "piggy sound" because it stands for i-i-i, a sound that reminds you of a squealing baby pig (refer to the movie "Babe" when the pig is calling for his mother).

2. Let students pretend to be "squealing little piglets" as they trace "i" onto the carpet.

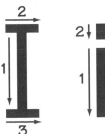

Word Construction

1. Ask the children to sort for the following letters (page 320):

s ĭ t b l f p n

2. Make the following words: <u>sit</u>, <u>bit</u>, <u>lit</u>, <u>fit</u>, <u>pit</u>, <u>pin</u>, <u>tin</u>, <u>fin</u>.

Blend, Read and Write

1. Blend and read:

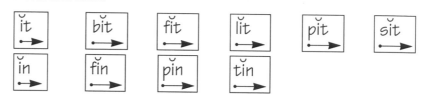

ĭt   bĭt   fĭt   lĭt   pĭt   sĭt

ĭn   fĭn   pĭn   tĭn

2. Write: The hat will fit him.

Books to Enhance Reading Comprehension, Skill and Language Development

Guided Reading:

<u>Monsters</u> - Andrea Butler (Rigby)

<u>My Twin</u> - Nora Fredericks (Modern Curriculum Press, <u>Ready Readers</u>)

Independent Reading:

Add <u>Roll Over</u> - Merle Peck (Houghton Mifflin)

<u>It Looked Like Spilt Milk</u> - Charles Shaw (Harper & Row, Big Book)

Writing Frame:

It looked like _____

but_____.

Make Your Own Little Books

<u>Will It Fit?</u>, pages 83-84. (Book 16)

Letter Cards for Word Construction (page 320)

Word Cards for Sentence Construction (page 321)

Words to Practice

will   it
yes   bit
no   fit
           pit
           sit

16

Will It Fit?

Name _____

8

1

✂ - ✂

Will it fit?

No!

6

3

No!

2

Yes, it fits!

7

Will it fit?

4

Reproducible

No!

5

Unit III
Lesson 5

Sight Vocabulary:

- Review <u>said</u>
- Introduce <u>as</u>
- Phonics and Structural Analysis: /h/; "z" sound for "s" (has, his)

Spelling: as, has, is his, at hat

Developing Phonemic Awareness

Read Aloud:

<u>Herman the Helper</u> - Robert Kraus (Scholastic, <u>Literacy Place</u>)

<u>Oh, A-Hunting We Will Go</u> - John Langstaff (Atheneum)

<u>A House Is a House for Me</u> - Mary Ann Hoberman (Scholastic)

Shared Reading:

<u>The Hobyahs</u> - Brenda Parkes (Rigby, Big Book)

Rhymes:

"Humpty Dumpty" - Mother Goose

"Hey, Diddle Diddle" - Mother Goose

Song:

"Ha - Ha Thisaway" - Raffi in <u>Everything Grows</u> (MCA)

Direct Instruction: /h/

1. Show the children the letter "Hh." Tell them you think of this as "the tired letter" because the sound it represents reminds you of the panting of a person who is out of breath: h-h-h.

2. Invite the children to "run in place." When you give the signal they are to stop and make the "h" sound.

3. Trace the lower case "h" onto the carpet while making its sound.

Unit III
Lesson 5

Blend, Read and Write

1. Blend and read:

ham →	hot →	hat →	him →	had →
hand →	hip →	has* →	his* →	

*Introduce "z" sound for "s."

Word Construction

1. Ask the children to sort for the following letters (page 322):

h	ă	t	ĭ	m	n	d	o	s

2. Make the following words: <u>hat</u>, <u>ham</u>, <u>him</u>, <u>hit</u>, <u>hot</u>, <u>hand</u>, <u>his</u>, <u>has</u>.

Books to Enhance Reading Comprehension, Skill and Language Development

Guided Reading:

<u>Happy Birthday!</u> - Avelyn Davidson (Rigby)

<u>How to Make a Hen House</u> - Bill Holly (Modern Curriculum Press, <u>Ready Readers</u>)

<u>I Hunter</u> - Pat Hutchins (Greenwillow)

Independent Reading:

Add <u>Monsters</u> - Andrea Butler (Rigby)

Activity for Home or School:

Make a house out of the letter <u>H</u>.

Writing Frame:

I had a _____.

It _____.

Make Your Own Little Books

<u>The Birthday Party</u>, pages 87-88. (Book 17)

Letter Cards for Word Construction (page 322)

Word Cards for Sentence Construction (page 323)

Words to Practice

the	it
is	bit
his	fit
and	hit
a	lit
	pit
	sit

8

The Birthday Party

Name _____

1

ice cream.
It is his

6

presents and . . .

3

Dan has balloons and . . .

2

birthday!

7

✂ - ✂

cards and . . .

4

a cake and . . .

5

Unit III
Lesson 6

Sight Vocabulary:

- Introduce: <u>go</u>
- Phonics and Structural Analysis: /g/ "hard g" goat

Spelling: go, pig, dig, big

Developing Phonemic Awareness

Read Aloud:

<u>Mr. Gumpy's Outing</u> - John Burningham (Holt)

Shared Reading:

<u>Greedy Cat's Breakfast</u> - Joy Cowley (Wright Group, Big Book)

<u>The Three Billy Goats Gruff</u> - Judith Smith and Brenda Parkes (Rigby, Big Book)

Rhymes:

"Goosey Goosey Gander" - Mother Goose

"There Was a Little Girl" - Mother Goose

Songs:

"Goober Peas" - Alan and Lea Daniel (Wright Group, Big Book and Tape)

"Goodbye" - Greg and Steve in <u>We All Live Together, Volume 1</u>, (Youngheart Records)

"He's Got the Whole World" - Raffi in <u>Rise and Shine</u> (A&M Records)

Direct Instruction: /g/

1. Show the children a sack of gum drops or gummy bears. Tell them "gum" begins with the letter <u>Gg</u> (Show letter). Explain that <u>Gg</u> represents two sounds, but today they will learn the "hard" sound: g-g-g.

2. Have the children place their fingers on their throats. Explain that the sound of "g" is made deep in the throat. Let them feel the vibration as they make this guttural sound.

Unit III
Lesson 6

Tip:

Draw children's attention to the letter "g" as it appears in print.

3. Use the pointer finger to trace the lower case "g" onto the carpet while making its sound.

4. Pass out gum drops to any child who can give you a word that begins with "g."

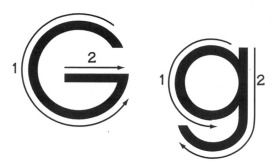

Working With Letters and Sounds

1. Ask the children to draw three adjacent squares called *soundboxes* on their chalkboards or papers.

2. Dictate the following words: <u>got</u>, <u>dog</u>, <u>dig</u>, <u>garden</u>, <u>give</u>, <u>pig</u>, <u>wig</u>, <u>get</u>. Ask the children to indicate the position of the "g" sound by writing the letter in the first or last box.

give | pig

Blend, Read, and Write

1. Blend and read:

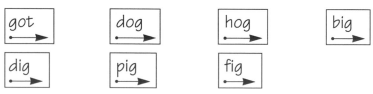

got   dog   hog   big
dig   pig   fig

2. Write: The dog can dig.

Word Construction

1. Ask the children to sort for the following letters (page 324):

g ŏ t h ĭ d f p b

2. Make the following words: <u>got</u>, <u>dog</u>, <u>hog</u>, <u>pig</u>, <u>dig</u>, <u>fig</u>, <u>big</u>, <u>pog</u>.

Books to Enhance Reading Comprehension, Skill and Language Development

Guided Reading:

<u>Good Night Gorilla</u> - Peggy Rathman (Putnam)

<u>Good Girl!</u> - Seth Jacobs (Modern Curriculum Press, <u>Ready Readers</u>)

<u>Growing Colors</u> - Bruce McMillan (Lothrop)

<u>Our Dog Sam</u> - Ron Bacon (Rigby)

Independent Reading:

Add <u>Happy Birthday!</u> - Avelyn Davidson (Rigby)

Make Your Own Little Books

<u>The Van</u>, pages 92-93. (Book 18)

<u>The Beach</u>, pages 94-95. (Book 18A)

Letter Cards for Word Construction (page 324)

Word Cards for Sentence Construction (page 325)

Unit III Evaluation

Directions:

Ask each child to read the lists of words and the sentence.

List A	List B
said	the
go	has
it	of
sit	to
his	got
if	like

Tim said, "I can go."

The boy, the girl, the man, and the baby got out of the van.

8

The Van

Name _____

1

 -

The bee got in the van.

6

The girl got in the van.

3

92

The boy got in the van.

2

Bz-z-z-z!

7

The man got in the van.

4

93
Reproducible

The baby got in the van.

5

Words to Practice

the	big
I	dig
in	fig
go	pig
to	
see	
like	

The Beach

Name _____

1

- -

I can go
to the food stand.

6

I can dig in the sand.

94
Reproducible

3 © Fearon Teacher Aids FE794

I like to go
to the beach.

2

I can go to see the boats.
I like the beach a lot!

7

I can swim.

4

I can sit in the sun.

5

95

© Fearon Teacher Aids FE7948

Unit IV

Target Word Recognition Skills:

/ĕ/, /j/, /k/, /q/, /w/, /x/, /y/, /z/, ē

are, saw, you, won't, have, these

**Unit IV
Lesson 1**

Sight Vocabulary:

- ■ Introduce: <u>are</u>
- ■ Phonics and Structural Analysis: /k/

Spelling: are, ask

Grammar, Mechanics and Usage:

Possessive <u>'s</u>; capital letter for person's name.

Developing Phonemic Awareness

Read Aloud:

<u>Koala Lou</u> - Mem Fox (Harcourt)

<u>Cookie's Week</u> - Cindy Word (Scholastic)

<u>Katy No-Pocket</u> - Emmy Payne (Houghton Mifflin)

<u>Where's Spot?</u> - Eric Hill (Putnam)

Shared Reading:

<u>The Three Little Kittens</u> - (Teacher-made Big Book)

Make a big book of the story of <u>The Three Little Kittens</u>. Share the story with the children.

Rhyme:

"I Had a Little Nut Tree" - Mother Goose

Song:

"BINGO" - Greg and Steve in <u>We All Live Together, Volume 4</u> (Youngheart Records) Substitute "K" and other letters. For example:

> There was a farmer
> Had a dog
> and KINGO was his name-o
> K - I - N - G - O
> K - I - N - G - O
> K - I - N - G - O
> And KINGO was his name-o.

Direct Instruction: /k/

1. Show the letter "Kk." Tell the children that it always reminds you of kisses (just as children begin to go "yuck," say "candy kisses"). Have a supply of candy kisses handy. Demonstrate the "k" sound. Remind children that the letter "c" also represents this sound.

Unit IV
Lesson 1

2. Pass out candy kisses to children who give you a word beginning with the "k" sound. Accept words spelled with "c," but write the words on the board so the children can see that many more words begin with "c."

K Words	C Words	
kitten	Cathy	cone
kitchen	Carl	cup
Kevin	can	careful
Kyle	come	color
	cucumber	

3. Ask the children to trace the lower case "k" onto the carpet as they make the "k" sound.

Working With Letters and Sounds

1. Ask the children to draw three adjacent squares called *soundboxes* on their chalkboards or papers.

2. Dictate the following words: <u>ask</u>, <u>kite</u>, <u>kitten</u>, <u>mask</u>, <u>task</u>, <u>kitchen</u>, <u>keep</u>, <u>pink</u>. Ask the students to indicate the position of the "k" sound by writing "k" in the first or last box.

      kite   pink

| k | | | | | | k |

Blend, Read and Write

1. Blend and read:

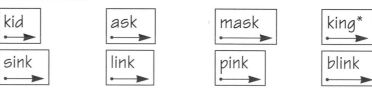

*the "ng" is a unique sound, but children don't have much trouble with it.

2. Write: The king has a mask.

Word Construction

1. Ask the children to sort for the following letters (page 326):

2. Make the following words: <u>ask</u>, <u>mask</u>, <u>pink</u>, <u>sink</u>, <u>king</u>, <u>bask</u>.

Unit IV
Lesson 1

Direct Instruction: are

■ positional words

1. Use a magnetic board, models, flannelboard, or overhead projector to show kittens in a house. Manipulate the "kittens" while saying:

    The kittens are on the couch.
    The kittens are behind the curtains.
    The kittens are under the bed.

2. Show the children how to make books. Ask them to draw their kittens (at least two) in a house. Tell them to hide their kittens under, behind or on top of some object. Each child should do one page.

3. As the children are drawing, cutting and pasting, walk around the room. Ask "Where are your kittens?" Write the child's answer below his or her picture, emphasizing the word are.

4. Bind the pages together to make a book. Choose a title.

Activity for Home or School

1. Give each child a card with the word are written on it.

2. Ask them to trace the word with crayon or glue. Take the card home to practice.

Books to Enhance Reading Comprehension, Skill and Language Development

Guided Reading:
Keep Out! - Will Hardy (Modern Curriculum Press, Ready Readers)
Keys - Mark Adams (Modern Curriculum Press, Ready Readers)
Kittens - Sherryl Jordan (Rigby)
Who Hid It? - Taro Gomi (Scholastic, Literacy Place)

Independent Reading:
Add Our Dog Sam - Ron Bacon (Rigby) and Where's Spot? - Eric Hill (Putnam)

Make Your Own Little Books:
Where Are the Kittens? pages 100-101. (Book 20)

Letter Cards for Word Construction (page 326)

Word Cards for Sentence Construction (page 327)

Words to Practice

are · · · · · ask
the · · · · · mask
on · · · · · · task
in
of
yes
no

Where Are the Kittens?

Name _____

8

1

Are the kittens on the couch? No.

6

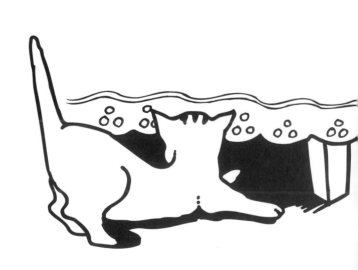

Are the kittens under the bed? No.

3

Where are the kittens?

2

Are the kittens in
the basket? Yes!

7

Are the kittens on top
of the table? No.

4

Are the kittens behind
the curtain? No.

5

© Fearon Teacher Aids FE7948

Unit IV Lesson 2

Sight Vocabulary:

- Review <u>are</u>
- Phonics and Structural Analysis: /ī/, i-e phonograms: _ike, _ide

Spelling: like, bike, hike, Mike, ride, side, tide, hide

Grammar, Mechanics and Usage:
Review conventions already introduced; adding "s" (likes)

Developing Phonemic Awareness

Read Aloud:

<u>Bo and Peter</u> - Betsy Franco (Scholastic, <u>Literacy Place</u>)
<u>Things I Like</u> - Anthony Browne (Random House)
<u>What Do You Like?</u> - Michael Grejniec (North-South Books)

Shared Reading:

Rhymes and Poems:
"Banbury Cross" - Mother Goose
"Three Blind Mice" - Mother Goose
"I Like Bugs . . ." - Margaret Wise Brown in <u>Fish With the Deep Blue Smile</u> (Dutton)

Song:
"Apples and Bananas" - Raffi in <u>One Light One Sun</u> (MCA)

Direct Instruction : /i/, i-e

1. Show the letter "Ii." Tell the children they have already learned one sound: ĭ. The sound they will learn today is very easy because the sound is the same as the letter name: ī. This is called the long sound.

2. Draw three adjacent boxes on the board:

Ask the children to spell the word "ride." Say, "What sound do you hear first?" Write the "r" in the first box.

r		

Ask, "What sound do you hear next?" Write down the "i" with the macron over it.

r	ī	

Tip:
The children might not realize that the "short" vowel sound (sit) is said quickly, while the "long" sound takes longer to say (site).

Unit IV
Lesson 2

Tip:

There are many different ways of presenting this concept. The method is not important, but the children <u>must</u> understand that although "ride" has four letters, the word is comprised of <u>three</u> phonemes. Research tells us that this is a crucial understanding.

Continue with "What sound do you hear at the end?" Write the "d" in the third box .

r	ī	d

Say "This word is spelled with an 'e' at the end. The 'e' signals the 'i' to say its long sound, but it does not represent a sound that you can hear. So I will put the 'e' in the last box, but put a broken line through it to remind us that the 'e' is 'silent.'"

r	ī	d e̸

3. Give other examples of words: side, like, bike.

Working With Letters and Sounds

1. Ask the children to draw three adjacent squares called *soundboxes* on their chalkboards or papers:

2. Dictate the following words. Remind the children to write the final "e" in the third box: <u>hike</u>, <u>bike</u>, <u>like</u>, <u>Mike</u>, <u>hide</u>, <u>ride</u>, <u>side</u>, <u>tide</u>.

Blend, Read, and Write

1. Blend and read:

līke̸ bīke̸ Mīke̸

hīde̸ rīde̸ sīde̸

2. Write: Mike has a red bike.

Books to Enhance Reading Comprehension, Skill and Language Development

Guided Reading:

<u>I Like</u> - Andrea Butler (Rigby)
<u>It Looked Like Spilt Milk</u> - Charles G. Shaw (Harper & Row)
<u>Little Kittens</u> - Mary Solis (Modern Curriculum Press, <u>Ready Readers</u>)

Independent Reading:

Add <u>Kittens</u> - Sherryl Jordan (Rigby)

Make Your Own Books:

<u>Mike and Ann</u>, pages 104-105. (Book 21)

Letter Cards for Word Construction (page 328)

Word Cards for Sentence Construction (page 329)

103

Words to Practice

are	bike
to	Mike
and	ride
on	side
like	tide

Mike and Ann

Name _____

8

1

Mike and Ann are in the big blue boat.

6

Mike and Ann like to ride the bikes.

3

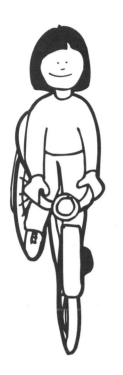

Mike and Ann are on red
and blue bikes.

2

Mike and Ann are sick.
Mike and Ann do **not** like
to ride in the boat.

7

Mike and Ann are on
the big, black train.

4

Mike and Ann like to
ride the train.

5

Unit IV
Lesson 3

Sight Vocabulary:

- Introduce <u>saw</u>, <u>these</u>
- Phonics and Structural Analysis: /w/, /ē/, be, <u>be</u>, <u>me</u>, <u>we</u>

Spelling: be, he, me, we, saw

Grammar, Mechanics and Usage:
Possessive 's; question and answer

Developing Phonemic Awareness

Read Aloud:
<u>Cookie's Week</u> - Cindy Ward (Scholastic)
<u>The Wind Blew</u> - Pat Hutchins (Scholastic)
<u>Whistle for Willie</u> - Ezra Jacks Keats (Puffin)

Shared Reading:
<u>Mrs. Wishy-Washy</u> - Joy Cowley (Wright Group)
<u>I Went Walking</u> - Sue Williams (Harcourt, Big Book)
<u>What Will the Weather Be Like Today?</u> - Paul Rogers (Greenwillow)

Rhymes and Poems:
"Wee Willie Winkie" - Mother Goose
"This Little Pig Went to Market" - Mother Goose

Song:
"The Eensy Weensy Spider" (Wright Group, Big Book and cassette)

Direct Instruction: /w/

1. Show the children the letter <u>Ww</u>. Tell them that it represents the sound they hear at the beginning of the words <u>water</u>, <u>wait</u>, <u>wagon</u> and <u>weather</u>. Draw their attention to the formation of your mouth as you make this sound.

2. Tell the children that you are going to recite some words. Every time they hear a word that begins with "w" they should raise their hands. If the word does not begin with "w" they should make a "no" gesture with their heads. Encourage the children to listen carefully and watch your lips as you say the following words: <u>walk</u>, <u>yellow</u>, <u>woman</u>, <u>weak</u>, <u>talk</u>, <u>were</u>, <u>witch</u>, <u>wallet</u>, <u>tooth</u>, <u>yell</u>, <u>under</u>, <u>waist</u>, <u>want</u>, <u>wind</u>.

106

Unit IV
Lesson 3

3. Ask the children to trace the lower case "w" onto the carpet as they make its sound.

Blend, Read and Write

1. Blend and read:

| wē* | bē | hē | mē |

| week | see | peek |

*Review the long ē sound.

2. Write: We went to see Tom.

Word Construction

1. Ask the children to sort for the following letters (page 330):

| w | k | b | m | h | p | e | e | s |

2. Make these words: we, he, be, me, week, seek, peek, meek.

Books to Enhance Reading Comprehension, Skill and Language Development

Guided Reading:
What Will the Weather Be Like Today? - Paul Rogers (Greenwillow)
All Wet - Judy Nayer (Modern Curriculum Press, Ready Readers)

Independent Reading:
Add The Birthday Cake - (Rigby)

Make Your Own Little Books
The Woods, pages 109-110. (Book 22)

Letter Cards for Word Construction (page 330)

Word Cards for Sentence Construction (page 331)

Unit IV
Lesson 3

Activity for Home or School

1. Reread <u>I Went Walking</u> by Sue Williams. Take a walk with the children and talk about the things you see. Back in the room have the children practice this dialogue with partners:

> Child #1: "I went walking."
> Child #2: "What did you see?"
> Child #1: "I saw_____."

2. Write down each pair's dialogue. Ask them to illustrate and write their names at the bottom. Bind the pages into a book. Draw attention to the word <u>saw</u>, as well as punctuation.

"I went walking," said Juan.

"What did you see?" asked Jose.

"I saw a bird," answered Juan.

Tip:
Have a parent sign the back of the card.

Activity for Home or School: saw
Give each child a card with the word "saw" written on it. Have them trace the word with crayon or glue. Take it home to practice. Add "saw" to the sight word collection.

Words to Practice

saw	we
a	me
to	be
the	he

The Woods

Name _____

8

1

We saw insects.

6

We saw squirrels.

3

109
Reproducible

© Fearon Teacher Aids FE7948

We went to the woods.

2

We saw a snake!

7

We saw birds.

4

We saw flowers.

5

Unit IV
Lesson 4

Sight Vocabulary:

- ■ Review <u>are</u>
- ■ Phonics and Structural Analysis: /ĕ/ phonograms: _en, _ed

Spelling: red, bed, fed, led, hen, men, pen, ten

Grammar, Mechanics and Usage:
Capitalizing a person's name; "s" for plural

Developing Phonemic Awareness

Read Aloud:

<u>The Elves and the Shoemaker</u> - Freya Littledale (Scholastic)

<u>The Elephant and the Bad Baby</u> - Elfrida Vipont (Coward - McCann)

<u>Ten in a Bed</u> - (Discovery Toys)

<u>Red is Best</u> - Kathy Swinson (Annick)

<u>Heckedy Peg</u> - Audrey Wood (Harcourt)

<u>Ten, Nine, Eight</u> - Molly Bang (Greenwillow)

Shared Reading:

<u>An Egg Is an Egg</u> - Micki Weiss (Harcourt <u>Signatures</u>, Big Book)

<u>Little Elephant</u> - Tana Hoban (Harcourt <u>Signatures</u>, Big Book)

<u>Who's in the Shed?</u> - Brenda Parkes (Rigby, Big Book)

<u>The Little Red Hen</u> - Brenda Parkes (Rigby, Big Book)

Rhymes and Poems:

"E is the Escalator" - Phyllis McGinley in <u>Poems to Read to the Very Young</u> (Random House)

"The Elephant" - Arnold Sundgaurd in <u>Animals, Animals</u> by Eric Carle (Philomel)

Songs:

"Little Sir Echo" - Greg and Steve in <u>We All Live Together, Volume I</u> (Youngheart Records)

"Everything Grows" - Raffi in <u>Everything Grows</u> (MCA)

Unit IV
Lesson 4

Direct Instruction: /ĕ/

1. Show the letter "Ee." Tell the children that they will learn the short sound represented by "Ee."

2. As you make the "ĕ" sound for the children, trace around your lips with your index and forefingers. Invite the children to do the same. Explain that this is the sound you hear at the beginning of <u>elephant</u> - ĕ ĕ ĕlephant.

3. Ask the children to trace the lower case "e" onto the carpet as they make the "ĕ" sound.

Working With Letters and Sounds

1. Ask the children to draw three adjacent squares called *soundboxes* on their chalkboards or papers.

2. Say, "Listen to the word *red*. What letter do you hear at the beginning?" Direct the children to write the letter <u>r</u> in the first box.

r		

3. "Listen to the word again - <u>red</u>. What letter do you hear at he end of the word?" Direct the children to write a "d" in the third box.

r		d

4. "Listen again: <u>red</u> (draw out the middle sound). What sound do you hear in the middle of the word?" Direct the children to write an "e" in the middle box.

r	e	d

5. Continue to repeat this procedure with the following words: <u>men</u>, <u>ten</u>, <u>bed</u>, <u>Ted</u>, <u>led</u>, <u>met</u>, <u>set</u>, <u>get</u>. Do it <u>with</u> the children.

Unit IV
Lesson 4

Blend, Read and Write

1. Blend and read:

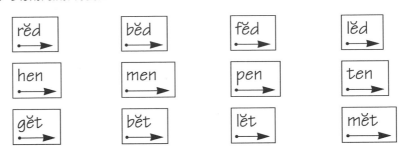

rĕd   bĕd   fĕd   lĕd

hen   men   pen   ten

gĕt   bĕt   lĕt   mĕt

2. Write: Ben has a red bed.

Word Construction

1. Ask the children to sort for the following letters (page 332):

e   t   n   d   r   T   B   s   m   b

2. Make the following words: ten, men, Ben, bed, red, Ted, met, set, net, send.

Books to Enhance Reading Comprehension, Skill and Language Development

Guided Reading:

The Birthday Cake - Andrea Butler (Rigby)

Going Fishing - Polly Peterson (Modern Curriculum Press, Ready Readers)

Independent Reading:

Add I Like - Andrea Butler (Rigby)

Ten in a Bed - (Discovery Toys)

Writing Frame:

The little red hen _____.

Make Your Own Little Books

The Zoo Keepers, pages 114-115. (Book 23)

Letter Cards for Word Construction (page 332)

Word Cards for Sentence Construction (page 333)

Tip:
Encourage the child to write as much as he or she can, using phonetic spelling.

113

Words to Practice

Ed	let
Ted	pet
fed	met
the	saw

The Zoo Keepers

Name _____

8

1

The men let Ted
feed the goats.

6

Ed saw the men feed
the elephants.

3

Ed and Ted saw the men
at the zoo.

2

The men let Ed and Ted
pet the lambs.
Ed and Ted like the Zoo!

7

Ted saw the men feed
the bears.

4

115
Reproducible

The men let Ed feed
the chickens.

5 © Fearon Teacher Aids FE7948

Sight Vocabulary:

- Review <u>of</u>, <u>are</u>, <u>to</u>, <u>saw</u>
- Introduce <u>you</u>, <u>won't</u>
- Phonics and Structural Analysis: /ō/, ōa, won't

Spelling: you, go, no, so, boat, goat, coat, go, no, so

Grammar, Mechanics and Usage:
The comma after "no," the exclamation and exclamation point.

Developing Phonemic Awareness

Read Aloud:
<u>OH!</u> - Josse Goffin (Harry Abrams)
<u>Mr. Gumpy's Outing</u> - John Burningham (Holt)

Shared Reading:
<u>A Mother for Choco</u> - Keiko Kasza (Houghton Mifflin, <u>Invitations to Literacy</u>, Big Book)
<u>Oh No!</u> - (Rigby, Big Book)

Rhymes and Poems:
"Little Jumping Joan" - Mother Goose
"Here We Go" - Mary Ann Hoberman in <u>Yellow Butter, Purple Jelly, Red Jam, Black Bread</u> (Viking)

Songs:
"Apples and Bananas" - Raffi in <u>One Light, One Sun</u> (MCA)
"Row, Row, Row Your Boat" - Raffi in <u>Rise and Shine</u> (Troubadour Records Ltd.)

Direct Instruction: /ō/

1. Show the children the letter <u>Oo</u>. Tell them they will learn the long sound of the letter ō. Explain that you think of this as "the surprised sound" of ō because people often say "Oh" when they are surprised. Let everyone say "Oh" as they throw up their hands in surprise.

2. Explain that when "o" and "a" are together they almost always stand for the long ō sound (bōat, cōat, gōat) .

Unit IV Lesson 5

Working With Letters and Sounds

1. Make three adjacent squares called *soundboxes* on the chalkboard.

2. Say the word <u>boat</u>. Show the children how the "b" goes in the first box, the ōa in the second box (one sound) and the "t" in the third box.

3. Ask the children to make their own boxes. Do the following words together: <u>coat</u>, <u>goat</u>, <u>toad</u>, <u>road</u>.

Blend, Read and Write

1. Blend and read:

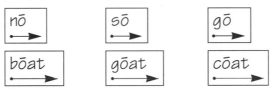

Word Construction

1. Ask the children to sort for the following letters (page 334):

b	a	t	g	c	l	r	o	d

2. Make the following words: <u>boat</u>, <u>coat</u>, <u>goat</u>, <u>toad</u>, <u>load</u>, <u>road</u>.

Books to Enhance Reading Comprehension, Skill and Language Development

Guided Reading:

"The Boat" - James Marshall in <u>Beginning to Read, Book A</u> (Houghton Mifflin)

<u>What Can Float</u> - Judy Sperack (Modern Curriculum Press, <u>Ready Readers</u>)

Independent Reading:

Add <u>What Will the Weather Be Like Today?</u> - Paul Rogers (Greenwillow)

<u>I Went Walking</u> - Sue Williams (Harcourt, Big Book)

Writing Frame:

I can go on a _____.

It _____.

Make Your Own Little Books:

<u>Oh, No!</u> pages 118-119. (Book 24)

Letter Cards for Word Construction (page 334)

Word Cards for Sentence Construction (page 335)

Words to Practice

no   won't
go   the
boat
coat

Oh, No!

Name _____

8   1

✂ - ✂

The motorcycle **can** go!

Oh, no!
The bus won't go!

6

118
Reproducible

3

Oh, no!
The car won't go!

2

We can go!

7

Oh, no!
The train won't go!

4

Oh, no!
The plane won't go!

5

Unit IV
Lesson 6

Sight Vocabulary:

- Review <u>of</u>, <u>are</u>, <u>to</u>, <u>saw</u>
- Phonics and Structural Analysis: /ks/, x, fox, box, six, fix, mix

Spelling: fox, box, six, fix. mix

Grammar, Mechanics and Usage:
Capitalization of a person's name

Developing Phonemic Awareness

Read Aloud:

<u>Where the Wild Things Are</u> - Maurice Sendak (Harper & Row)
<u>My Cat Likes to Hide in Boxes</u> - Eve Sutton (Parents Magazine Press)
<u>What's Inside the Box?</u> - Ethel & Leonard Kessler (Dodd, Mead)

Shared Reading:

<u>Hattie and the Fox</u> - Mem Fox (Big Book)

Rhyme:

"Mix a Pancake" - Christina Rossetti in <u>Read-Aloud Rhymes for the Very Young</u> (Alfred A. Knopf)

Direct Instruction: ks Xx

1. Show the letter <u>Xx.</u> Say, "Poor <u>Xx</u>. It has no sound of its own. It stands for the same sound that three other letters have -<u>cks</u>, as in <u>socks</u>. So we spell 'socks' s-o-c-k-s, but we spell 'box' b-o-x. How do you think "fox" is spelled?" Do the same with <u>ax</u>, <u>tax</u>, <u>Max</u>, <u>six</u>, <u>mix</u>.

2. Write the word <u>exit</u> on the chalkboard. Challenge the children to find the word <u>exit</u> in the classroom. Discuss its meaning.

Blend, Read and Write

1. Blend and read:

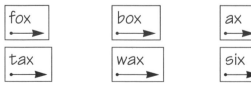

| fox → | box → | ax → | Max → |
| tax → | wax → | six → | mix → |

2. Write: Max had a big box.

Unit IV
Lesson 6

Tip:

Have each child hide a small object in a box or a bag. Ask him or her to write clues so the other kids can guess what he or she has hidden.

Word Construction

1. Ask the children to sort for the following letters (page 336):

| x | *b* | o | f | a | M | i | m | s | t | w |

2. Make these words: Max, ax, tax, wax, box, fox, six, mix.

Books to Enhance Reading Comprehension, Skill and Language Development

Guided Reading:

A Big, Big Box - Rebecca Heber (Modern Curriculum Press, Ready Readers)

A Toy Box - Andrea Butler (Rigby)

Independent Reading:

Add "The Boat" - James Marshall in Beginning to Read, Book A (Houghton Mifflin)

Writing Frame:

It is [round].

It can [bounce].

It [is a toy].

What is it?

Make Your Own Little Books:

What's in the Box? pages 122-123. (Book 25)

Letter Cards for Word Construction (page 336)

Word Cards for Sentence Construction (page 337)

Words to Practice

box   fox
of   in
the   It's
a

What's in the Box?

Name _____

1

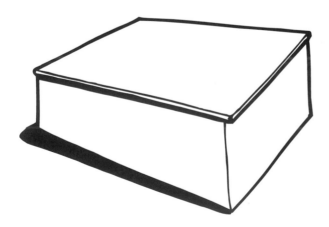

What's in the box?

6

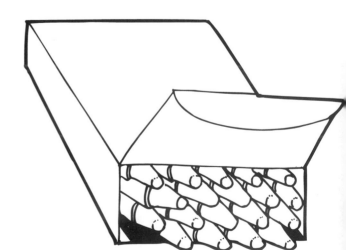

It's a box of crayons!

3

122
Reproducible

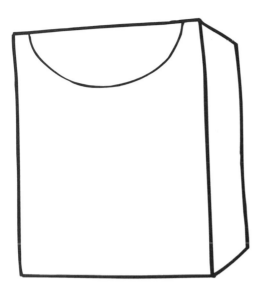

What's in the box?

2

It's a box of toy cars!

7

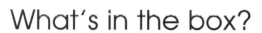

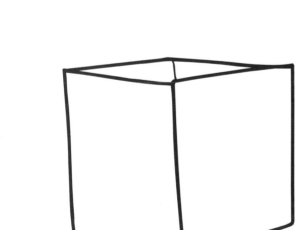

What's in the box?

4

123
Reproducible

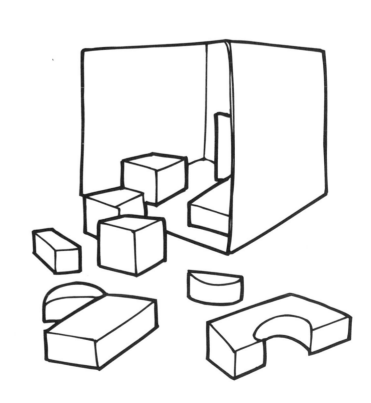

It's a box of blocks!

5

Unit IV
Lesson 7

Sight Vocabulary:

- Review <u>of</u>, <u>are</u>, <u>to</u>, <u>saw</u>
- Phonics and Structural Analysis: /j/
- Phonogram _ill.

Spelling: Jill, hill, fill, Bill, mill, will, pill

Mechanics and Usage:

Capitalization of a person's name; the exclamation point.

Developing Phonemic Awareness

Read Aloud:

<u>Julius, the Baby of the World</u> - Kevin Henkes (Morrow)

<u>No Jumping on the Bed</u> - Tedd Arnold (Dial)

<u>Norma Jean, Jumping Bean</u> - Joanna Cole (Random House)

Shared Reading:

<u>Jump, Frog, Jump!</u> - Robert Kalan (Greenwillow).

<u>The Jigaree</u> - Joy Cowley (Wright Group, Big Book)

<u>Jack and the Beanstalk</u> - Judith Smith and Brenda Parkes (Rigby, Big Book)

Rhymes:

"Jack and Jill" - Mother Goose

"Jack Be Nimble" - Mother Goose

"Little Jumping Joan" - Mother Goose

Song:

"John Jacob Jingleheimer Schmidt" - See <u>Juba This and Juba That</u> by Virginia A. Trashjian (Little, Brown & Company) p. 106.

Tip:

This is a good time to let children know that there are different ways of writing letters.

Direct Instruction: /j/

1. Show the letter "Jj." Tell the children that it stands for the sound at the beginning of many people's names: <u>Jesse</u>, <u>James</u>, <u>Jennifer</u>, <u>Jessica</u>, <u>Jonathan</u>, <u>Jeffrey</u>, <u>Jason</u> and <u>Jill</u>.

2. Trace lower case "j" while making the "j" sound.

124

Unit IV
Lesson 7

Blend, Read and Write

1. Blend and read:

 Jŏn   Jĭll   jăm   Jĭm

jĕt Jĕss jĕll

2. Write: Jim got on the jet .

Books to Enhance Reading Comprehension, Skill and Language Development

Guided Reading:

Jan Can Juggle - Kate McGovern (Modern Curriculum Press, Ready Readers)

Jack-In-The-Box - Andrea Butler (Rigby)

"Just Like Daddy" - Frank Asch in Beginning to Read, Book A (Houghton Mifflin)

Independent Reading:

Add A Toy Box - Andrea Butler (Rigby)

Mrs. Wishy-Washy - Joy Cowley (Wright Group)

Activity for Home or School: Make a flip book

Write the word "Bill" on an index card or use the activity sheet provided on page 126. On pieces of paper large enough to cover the first letter, write f, d, h, k, m, p, s, t, w. Staple these papers to the card to make a "flip book" to use for initial consonant substitution.

Make Your Own Little Books:

Jack and Jill, pages 127-128. (Book 26)

Word Cards for Sentence Construction (page 338)

Flip Book

Directions: Reproduce on construction paper. Have children cut the pieces out. Staple letters to cover the "B" in Bill to make flip books.

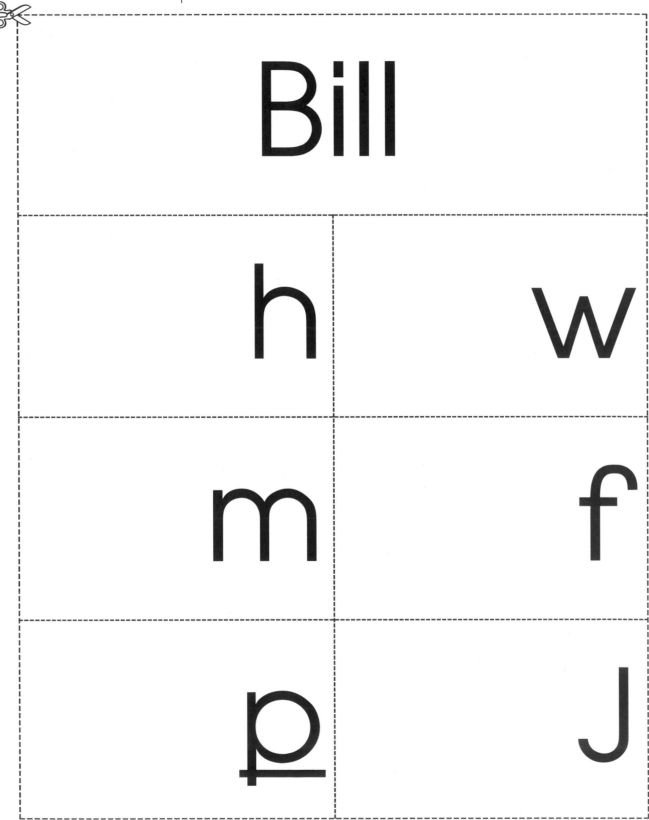

Reproducible

Words to Practice

and	Bill
went	hill
the	Jill
to	mill
his	pill
a	will
	still

Jack and Jill

Name _____

8

1

And broke his crown

6

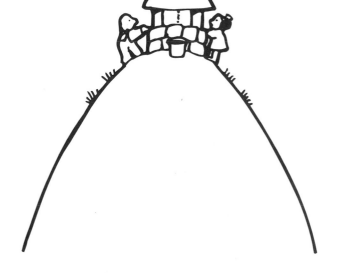

went up the hill.

3

Jack and Jill

2

And Jill came
tumbling after,

7

to fetch a pail of water.

4

Jack fell down

5

Unit IV
Lesson 8

Sight Vocabulary:

- Review <u>of</u>, <u>are</u>, <u>to</u>, <u>saw</u>
- Introduce <u>you</u>, <u>yes</u>
- Phonics and Structural Analysis: /y/ phonogram _et; bet, get, jet, let, met, net, pet, wet, yet

Spelling: yes, yet, bet, get, let, jet, met, pet, wet

Grammar and Mechanics and Usage:
Comma after "yes" and "no."

Developing Phonemic Awareness

Read Aloud:

<u>Yo! Yes!</u> - Chris Raschka (Orchard)

<u>Yes</u> - Josse Goffin (Lothrop)

<u>Little Blue and Little Yellow</u> - Leo Lionni (Astor - Honor)

<u>Purple, Green and Yellow</u> - Robert Munsh (Annick Press)

Shared Reading:

<u>Yankee Doodle</u> - Alan Daniel (The Wright Group)

<u>Yes, Ma'am</u> - June Melser (The Wright Group)

Rhymes and Poems:

"Yellow" - David McCord in <u>Poems to Read to the Very Young</u> (Random House)

Song:

"Yankee Doodle" - Alan Daniel (The Wright Group)

Direct Instruction: /y/

1. Show the letter <u>Yy</u>. Tell the children that it represents the sound they hear at the beginning of <u>yellow</u>, <u>yo-yo</u>, <u>yes</u>, <u>you</u>, and <u>yesterday</u>.

2. Trace lower case "y" onto the carpet while making the "y" sound.

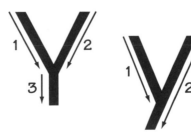

Unit IV
Lesson 8

Blend, Read, and Write

1. Blend and read:

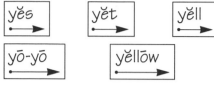

yĕs →   yĕt →   yĕll →   yăk →

yō-yō →   yĕllōw →

2. Write: Yes, I can get a yo-yo.

Word Construction

1. Ask the children to sort for the following letters (page 339):

y   e   s   t   b   m   w   s   n   j

2. Make these words: <u>yet</u>, <u>set</u>, <u>met</u>, <u>bet</u>, <u>wet</u>, <u>net</u>, <u>jet</u>, <u>yes</u>.

Books to Enhance Reading Comprehension, Skill and Language Development

Guided Reading:

<u>Do You Want to Be My Friend?</u> - Eric Carle (Harper)

<u>Have You Seen My Cat?</u> - Eric Carle (Picture Book Studio)

<u>Have You Seen My Duckling?</u> - Nancee Tafuri (Greenwillow)

<u>Yellow Ball</u> - Molly Bang (Morrow)

<u>Zebra's Yellow Van</u> - Diane Phillips (Modern Curriculum Press, <u>Ready Readers</u>)

Independent Reading:

Add <u>Jack-in-the-Box</u> - Andrea Butler (Rigby)

Writing Frame:

I can get a <u>[pencil]</u>.

I can get a <u>[book]</u>.

I can get a <u>[toy]</u>.

but I <u>can't</u> get a <u>[tiger]</u>.

Make Your Own Little Books:

<u>Will You Help?</u> pages 131-132. (Book 27)

Letter Cards for Word Construction (page 339)

Word Cards for Sentence Construction (page 340)

Tip:

Do the writing frame activity orally using a pocket chart for the children's responses to the question: "What can you get?"

130

Oh, yes, you will!
Go to bed!

8

Will You Help?

Name _____

1

Jan, will you go to bed?

6

No, I won't!

3

Jan, will you feed
the cat?

2

No, I won't!

7

Jan, will you get
the baby?

4

No, I won't!

5

Unit IV Lesson 9

Sight Vocabulary:

- Review <u>of</u>, <u>are</u>, <u>to</u>, <u>you</u>, <u>saw</u>
- Introduce <u>have</u>
- Phonics and Structural Analysis: /v/
- Phonogram: _an; can, Dan, fan, man, Nan, pan, ran, tan, van

Spelling: an, can, Dan, fan, man, Nan, pan, ran, tan, van, have

Grammar, Mechanics and Usage: Letter writing

Developing Phonemic Awareness

Read Aloud:

<u>The Very Busy Spider</u> - Eric Carle (Philomel)

<u>Mama, Do You Love Me?</u> - Barbara Joosse (Chronicle)

Shared Reading:

<u>The Very Young Hungry Caterpillar</u> - Eric Carle (Philomel)

Rhyme:

"There Was a Little Girl" - Mother Goose

Song:

L-O-V-E from <u>Music Is Magic</u> - Nellie Edge and Tom Hunter (Nellie Edge Enterprises)

Direct Instruction: /v/

1. Show the letter <u>Vv</u>. Tell the children that you can feel the vibrations when you make the sound this letter represents. Press your fingers against your lips as you make the "v" sound. Invite the children to do the same.

2. Trace lower case "v" onto the carpet, while making its sound.

Working With Letters and Sounds

1. Ask the children to draw three adjacent squares called soundboxes on their chalkboards or papers.

Unit IV
Lesson 9

2. Dictate the following words: <u>van</u>, <u>vet</u>, <u>love</u>, <u>have</u>, <u>give</u>, <u>live</u>.

3. Help the children to write the beginning, ending and medial letters representing their respective sounds. If an "e" is at the end, remind the children that this letter is often "silent."

live

| l | i | v̆e̸ |

Blend, Read, and Write

1. Blend and read:

| ăn → | văn → | băn → | căn → | Dăn → | făn → | măn → |

2 Write: Dan is in the red van.

Word Construction

1. Ask the children to sort for the following letters (page 341):

| a | c | D | f | m | <u>n</u> | <u>p</u> | N |

2. Make the words: <u>an</u>, <u>can</u>, <u>fan</u>, <u>Dan</u>, <u>man</u>, <u>Nan</u>, <u>pan</u>, <u>van</u>.

Books to Enhance Reading Comprehension, Skill and Language Development

Guided Reading:

"Sleepy Bear" - Lydia Dabcovich in <u>Beginning to Read, Book A</u> (Houghton Mifflin)

<u>Very Big</u> - Cherie Horn (Modern Curriculum Press, <u>Ready Readers</u>)

<u>Zebra's Yellow Van</u> - Diane Phillips (Modern Curriculum Press, <u>Ready Readers</u>)

Independent Reading:

Add <u>Do You Want to Be My Friend?</u> - Eric Carle (Harper)

Writing Frame: Love Letters

Give the children the opportunity to write "love letters" to anyone they choose (page 135). Let them decorate their letters with symbols of love. Teach proper letter form and punctuation.

Date_____

Dear _____,

I love you very much.

You _____

Love,

_____

Make Your Own Little Books:

<u>The Red Van</u>, pages 136-137. (Book 28)

Letter Cards for Word Construction (page 341)

Word Cards for Sentence Construction (page 342)

Tip:

The classroom "mailbox" is one of the best ways to foster authentic writing. Let the children "mail" their letters to one another. Provide lots of markers, stickers, envelopes, etc.

Date _____

Dear _____,

I love you very much.

You _____

_____

_____.

Love,

_____

Words to Practice

have	an
saw	can
asked	Dan
like	fan
said	man
to	Nan
	pan
	ran
	tan

The Red Van

Name _____

8

1

"I like it," said Mom.
"Let's get it."

6

"Can we have it?"
asked Nan.

Dad and Nan saw a big red van.

2

Dad went to the man. He said, "We like the van. We will take it."

7

"We can ask Mom," said Dad.

4

"Mom, we like the red van. We want to get it," said Nan.

5

Sight Vocabulary:

- Review <u>of</u>, <u>are</u>, <u>to</u>, <u>saw</u>, <u>you</u>
- Introduce <u>too</u>
- Phonics and Structural Analysis: /z/ /oo/

Spelling: too, zoo, soon, moon

Developing Phonemic Awareness

Read Aloud:

<u>Zella, Zack and Zodiac</u> - Bill Peet (Houghton Mifflin)

<u>Zoophabets</u> - Robert Tallon (Scholastic)

<u>Zoom</u> - Istvan Banyai (Viking)

<u>Zomo the Rabbit</u> - Gerald McDermott (Harcourt)

<u>50 Below Zero</u> - Robert Munsch (Annick)

Shared Reading:

<u>Lazy Mary</u> - June Melser (Wright Group, Big Book)

Rhyme:

"The Beehive" (page 140)

Direct Instruction: /z/

1. Ask the children to pretend to go to sleep, and while they are "sleeping," encourage them to make "sleeping sounds."

2. Tell students that one of the sounds used to show a sleeping person is the sound represented by the letter "Zz" (show letter). Explain that artists often make a succession of <u>z</u>'s to indicate a sleeping person. Illustrate by drawing a picture on the board.

3. Ask the children to trace "z" onto the carpet while making the "z" sound.

Working With Letters and Sounds

1. Ask the children to draw three adjacent squares called soundboxes on their chalkboards or papers.

2. Dictate the following words: <u>zoo</u>, <u>zipper</u>, <u>fuzz</u>, <u>zone</u>, <u>because</u>, <u>zero</u>, <u>boys</u>, <u>pigs</u>.

Tip:

Remind the children that "s" often has the "z" sound, especially at the end of a word.

Unit IV
Lesson 10

3. Ask the children to indicate the position of the "z" sound by writing "z" in the first or last box. Remind them that the letter "s" often represents the "z" sound.

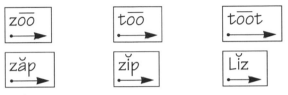

zoo

| z | | |

fuzz

| | | z |

Blend, Read and Write

1. Blend and read:

zōō →   tōō →   tōōt →

zăp →   zĭp →   Lĭz →

2. Write: Liz went to the zoo.

Word Construction

1. Ask the children to sort for the following letters (page 343):

| z | ōō | t | i | p | l | f | m | n |

2. Make these words: zōō, tōō, tōōl, pōōl, fōōl, mōōn, zōōm, zip.

Books to Enhance Reading Comprehension, Skill and Language Development

Guided Reading:

A Zoo - Andrea Butler (Rigby)

Good-bye Zoo - Bob Egan (Modern Curriculum Press, Ready Readers)

Toot Toot - Brian Wildsmith (Oxford University Press)

Dear Zoo - Red Campbell (Puffin)

Independent Reading:

Add 1,2,3 to the Zoo - Eric Carle (Philomel)

Lazy Mary - Jane Melser (Wright Group, Big Book)

Make Your Own Little Books:

At the Zoo, pages 141-142. (Book 29)

Letter Cards for Word Construction (page 343)

Word Cards for Sentence Construction (page 344)

139

The Beehive

Here is the beehive.

Where are the bees?

Hidden away where nobody sees.

Watch as they come out of their hive –

One,

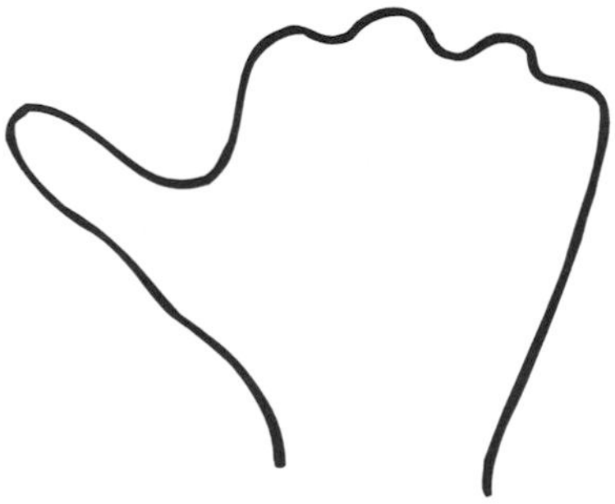

Two,

Three,

Four,

Five!

They're alive!

BZZZZZ!

Words to Practice

zoo   saw
too   to
        go
        did
        like
        go

At the Zoo

Name _____

8   1

✂ - ✂

I saw a hippo at the zoo.

I did, too!

6   **141**   3   © Fearon Teacher Aids FE7948

I saw a zebra at the zoo.

2

I did too! We like to go to the zoo!

7

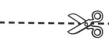

I saw a gorilla at the zoo.

4

I did, too!

5

Unit IV
Lesson 11

Sight Vocabulary:

- Review _of, are, to, saw, you, too_
- Phonics and Structural Analysis: /kw/ /qu/ phonogram _ick; quick, sick, kick, lick, tick

Spelling: quick, sick, kick, lick, pick, tick

Grammar, Mechanics and Usage: Question, question mark

Developing Phonemic Awareness

Read Aloud:

Q is for Duck - Mary Elting (Clarion)

Quick as a Cricket - Audrey Wood (Child's Play)

The Very Quiet Cricket - Eric Carle (Philomel)

Whatley's Quest - Bruce Whatley (Harper Collins)

The Quiet Book - Margaret Wise Brown (Harper Collins)

The Quilt Story - Tony Johnston (Putnam)

Shared Reading:

"The Pickety Fence" - David McCord in Everytime I Climb a Tree (Little, Brown)

"Queen of Hearts" - Mother Goose

Five Little Ducks - Ian Beck (Harcourt Invitations to Reading, Big Book)

Song:

"Six Little Ducks" - Raffi in More Singable Songs (MCA)

Direct Instruction: /kw/ q

1. Show the children the letter Qq. Tell them that it is similar to the letter "x" because it does not have a sound of its own. It sounds like two other letters: "k" and "w" - kw.

2. Tell the children that there is something else unusual about the letter "q." Ask them to try to guess what it is as you write these words on the board: queen, quiet, question, quilt, quills, quick. Give clues until someone notices that the "q" is always followed by "u."

© Fearon Teacher Aids FE7948

3. Trace "q" onto the carpet while making the "q" sound.

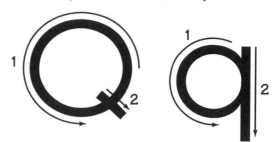

Working With Letters and Sounds

1. Ask the children to draw three adjacent squares called *soundboxes* on their chalkboards or papers.

2. Dictate the following words: <u>quiet</u>, <u>queen</u>, <u>quilt</u>, <u>question</u>, <u>quill</u>, <u>quip</u>, <u>quick</u>. Ask the children to spell the first and last sound they hear.

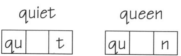

quiet | queen

| qu | | t | | qu | | n |

Blend, Read and Write

1. Blend and read:

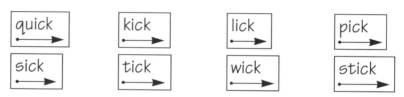

quick   kick   lick   pick

sick   tick   wick   stick

2. Write: Rick can kick the stick.

Word Construction

1. Ask the children to sort for the following letters (page 345):

q | u | i | l | s | R | w | t | k | p | c | k

2. Make the following words: <u>quick</u>, <u>lick</u>, <u>sick</u>, <u>Rick</u>, <u>wick</u>, <u>tick</u>, <u>kick</u>, <u>pick</u>.

Unit IV
Lesson 11

Books to Enhance Reading Comprehension, Skill and Language Development

Guided Reading:
When I Was Sick - Janet Hillman (Rigby)

The Green Queen - Nick Sharratt (Candlewick Press)

Independent Reading:
Add A Zoo - Andrea Butler (Rigby)

Toot Toot - Brian Wildsmith (Oxford University Press)

Writing Frame:
When I was sick I _____.

Make Your Own Little Books:
Mother, Mother, I Am Sick, pages 146-147. (Book 30)

Letter Cards for Word Construction (page 345)

Word Cards for Sentence Construction (page 346)

Unit IV Evaluation

Directions:
Ask each child to read the list of words and the sentence. Then ask the child to write: Nan saw the big cats at the zoo.

List A	List B
of	have
are	too
to	you
saw	won't
I	and

Dan saw a big green van.

Words to Practice

in	kick
the	lick
came	pick
said	sick
	quick

Mother,
Mother,
I Am Sick

Traditional

Name _____

8

1

"Nothing," said the lady

6

In came the doctor
In came the nurse
In came the lady
with the alligator purse.

3

Mother, Mother,
I am sick
Send for the doctor
quick, quick, quick.

2

with the alligator purse.

7

"Measles," said
the doctor.

4

147

"Mumps," said the nurse.

5

Unit V

Target Word Recognition Skills:

sh, wh, ch, th, ŭ

<u>my</u>, <u>come</u>, <u>do</u>, <u>they</u>, <u>want</u>, <u>put</u>, <u>what</u>, <u>here</u>, <u>good</u>, <u>hello</u>, <u>OK</u>, <u>don't</u>

Unit V
Lesson 1

Sight Vocabulary:

- Introduce <u>they</u>, <u>put</u>
- Phonics and Structural Analysis: /u/

Spelling: they, run, sun, fun, up, cup, but, cut nut

Grammar, Mechanics and Usage: Introduce "speech balloons"

Developing Phonemic Awareness

Read Aloud:

<u>Umbrella</u> - Taro Yashima (Viking)

<u>The Runaway Bunny</u> - Margaret Wise Brown (Harper & Row)

Shared Reading:

<u>The Ugly Duckling</u> - Hans Christian Andersen (Rigby, Big Book)

<u>The Bus Stop</u> - Nancy Hellen (Orchard)

Rhymes:

"Humpty Dumpty" - Mother Goose

"Rub-a-dub-dub" - Mother Goose

Songs:

"Five Little Ducks" - Raffi in <u>Rise and Shine</u> (Troubadour Records, Ltd.)

"Little White Duck" - Raffi in <u>Everything Grows</u> (MCA)

Direct Instruction: /ŭ/

1. Show the children the letter "Uu." Tell them it reminds you of an umbrella because you can see the "U" in the umbrella handle. Also, "umbrella" begins with "u."

2. Show the children how you can find the short sound of "u" by starting to say <u>umbrella</u>, but drawing out the first sound: <u>uuuumbrella</u>.

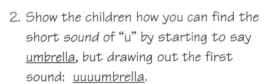

3. Write the word <u>umbrella</u> up the board. Say "This word starts with "u" also: <u>uuup</u>, <u>up</u>.

Another way to remember the sound is to pretend you are trying to open an umbrella that is stuck. As you make the motions, say "uh, uh, uh."

Unit V
Lesson 1

4. Tell the children that you will read some words. If the word begins with u, they should stand _up_; if it does not, they should remain _seated_. Read the following words: <u>under</u>, <u>eat</u>, <u>uncle</u>, <u>uphill</u>, <u>unhappy</u>, <u>act</u>, <u>napping</u>, <u>upstairs</u>, <u>rain</u>, <u>unknown</u>, <u>position</u>, <u>seat</u>, <u>underwear</u>.

5. Ask the children to trace "u" onto the carpet while making its short sound.

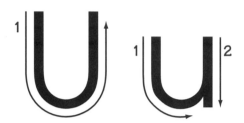

Working With Letters and Sounds

1. Ask the children to draw three adjacent squares called *soundboxes* on their chalkboards or papers.

2. Dictate the following words: <u>cup</u>, <u>run</u>, <u>sun</u>, <u>gum</u>, <u>tug</u>, <u>run</u>, <u>rub</u>, <u>tub</u>. Direct the children to record the beginning, middle and ending sounds in their squares.

cut

c	u	t

Blend, Read and Write

1. Blend and read:

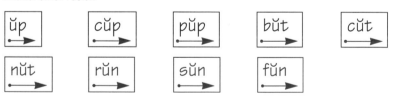

2. Write: The pup had fun in the sun.

Word Construction

1. Ask the children to sort for the following letters (page 347):

ŭ	c	t	n	f	s	b	r	m

2. Make the following words: <u>run</u>, <u>fun</u>, <u>sun</u>, <u>but</u>, <u>up</u>, <u>cup</u>, <u>us</u>, <u>must</u>.

Unit V
Lesson 1

Tip:

Help the children to see that although "put" does not have the short u sound, context clues will help with pronunciation. Example: "The girl pŭt on her new hat" does not make sense. Think and correct.
(Note: Mispronounce the word pŭt with a short u sound.)

Books to Enhance Comprehension, Skill and Language Development

Guided Reading:

<u>Dressing Up</u> - Dorothy Avery (Rigby)

<u>Good Night Little Bug</u> - Cynthia Rothman (Modern Curriculum Press, <u>Ready Readers</u>)

<u>A Nut Pie for Jud</u> - Emily Beth Gerard (Modern Curriculum Press, <u>Ready Readers</u>)

<u>Little House</u> - Polly Peterson (Modern Curriculum Press, <u>Ready Readers</u>)

Independent Reading:

Add <u>When I Was Sick</u> - Janet Hillman (Rigby)

Activity for Home or School: put, they

1. Distribute index cards with the words "they" and "put." Ask the children to trace over these words with crayons or glue.

2. Take these cards home for practice.

Writing Frame:

I saw _____.

They _____.

Make Your Own Little Books:

<u>Fruit Salad</u>, pages 152-153. (Book 31)

Letter Cards for Word Construction (page 347)

Word Cards for Sentence Construction (page 348)

Words to Practice

they	but
put	nut
in	up
the	cup
cut	pup

Fruit Salad

Name _____

8

1

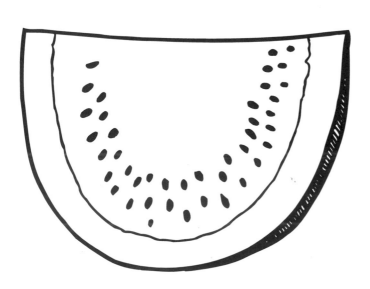

They cut up the watermelon. They put the watermelon in the bowl.

"Yes," said Mom. Jim and Matt cut up the apples. They put the apples in the bowl.

6

152

3

"Can we have
a fruit salad?" asked
Jim and Matt.

2

Jim and Matt have fruit
salad. They like it.

7

They cut up the bananas.
They put the bananas in
the bowl.

4

They cut up the oranges.
They put the oranges in
the bowl.

5

Unit V
Lesson 2

Sight Vocabulary:

- Review <u>they</u>, <u>put</u>
- Introduce <u>do</u>, <u>come</u>, <u>here</u>, <u>want</u>
- Phonics and Structural Analysis: /th/; don't, I'll; _ed (wanted)

Spelling: this, that, them, with

Grammar, Usage and Mechanics:

Review conventions; review past tense. Introduce comparative adjectives (big, bigger, biggest)

Developing Phonemic Awareness

Read Aloud:

<u>The Three Bears</u> - Paul Galdone (Scholastic)
<u>The Three Billy Goats Gruff</u> - Paul Galdone (Scholastic)
<u>The First Thanksgiving</u> - Jean Craighead George (Philomel)

Shared Reading:

<u>The Three Little Pigs</u> - Brenda Parkes (Rigby, Big Book)

Rhymes:

"Little Jack Horner" - Mother Goose
"Three Blind Mice" - Mother Goose

Song:

"Thanks a Lot" - Raffi in <u>Rise and Shine</u> (Troubadour Records, Ltd.)

Direct Instruction: /th/

1. Display the digraph <u>th</u>. Tell the children that you think of "th" as the "rude" letters for two reasons:

   1. When you make the <u>th</u> sound, you must stick out your tongue, which isn't very polite.

   2. When Little Jack Horner stuck his <u>thumb</u> in his pie, <u>he</u> wasn't very polite either.

Unit V
Lesson 2

2. Tell the children that they are going to pretend to be Little Jack Horner. Everyone will "stick in his or her thumb" and when they take it out, they'll say "th, th, th."

> Little Jack Horner
> Sat in a corner
> Eating his Christmas pie.
> He stuck in his thumb
> And pulled out a plum
> And said, "th, th, th!"

3. Trace "th" onto the carpet while making its sound. Make sure the children understand that these two letters represent <u>one sound</u>.

Working With Letters and Sounds

1. Ask the children to draw three adjacent squares called soundboxes on their chalkboards or papers.

2. Dictate the following words: <u>thank</u>, <u>teeth</u>, <u>with</u>, <u>them</u>, <u>think</u>, <u>thought</u>, <u>fifth</u>, <u>Thanksgiving</u>. Ask them to write "th" in the first or last box.*

thank

th		

with

		th

*Strictly speaking the "th" in <u>thank</u> and <u>them</u> do not have exactly the same sounds (voiced and unvoiced) but I haven't found it necessary to differentiate.

Blend, Read and Write

1. Blend and read:

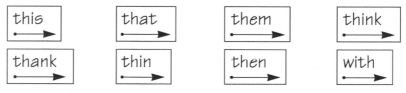

this →	that →	them →	think →
thank →	thin →	then →	with →

2. Write: Beth will go with you. This is for you.

Unit V
Lesson 2

Word Construction

1. Ask the children to sort for the following letters (page 349):

t	h	i	s	e	m	n	w	k	a	t

2. Make these words: <u>this</u>, <u>them</u>, <u>then</u>, <u>with</u>, <u>thin</u>, <u>think</u>, <u>that</u>, <u>thank</u>.

Books to Enhance Reading Comprehension, Skill and Language Development

Guided Reading:

"Come In, Boo Bear" - David McPhail in <u>Beginning to Read, Book A</u> (Houghton Mifflin)

<u>What Is This?</u> - Carly Easton (Modern Curriculum Press, <u>Ready Readers</u>)

Activity for Home or School

Have the children write the following sight words on index cards: <u>do</u>, <u>come</u>, <u>here</u>. Ask them to trace over their words with crayon and add to their sight word collection.

Writing Frame:

This is <u>[a picture of my pet]</u>.

It <u>[is a little goldfish]</u>.

Make Your Own Little Books:

<u>The Three Billy-Goats</u>, pages 157-158. (Book 32)

Letter Cards for Word Construction (page 349)

Word Cards for Sentence Construction (page 350)

And he did.

8

The Three Billy Goats

Name _____

1

"OK," said the troll.
"Be off with you."
The third billy goat went
up the hill. He wanted to

6

to eat you."
"No, no. Wait for
my brother. He is
much bigger."
"Ok," said the troll.
"Be off with you."

3

The first billy goat
went up the hill. He
wanted to get fat.
"Come here," said
the troll. "I want

2

get fat, too.
"I want to eat you,"
said the troll.
"I'll get you first," said
the third billy goat.

7

The second billy goat
went up the hill. He
wanted to get fat, too.
"I want to eat you,"

4

said the troll.
"No, no, wait for my
brother," said the
second billy goat.
"He is much bigger."

5

**Unit V
Lesson 3**

Sight Vocabulary:

- Review <u>do</u>, <u>come</u>, <u>hello</u>, <u>good</u>, <u>ok</u>
- Phonics and Structural Analysis: sh; <u>it's</u>, <u>I'll</u>, <u>can't</u>

Spelling: she, wish, fish dish

Grammar, Mechanics and Usage:
The apostrophe, the exclamation point and "speech balloons"

Developing Phonemic Awareness

Read Aloud:
<u>Sheep in a Jeep</u> - Nancy Shaw (Houghton Mifflin)
<u>Sheep in a Shop</u> - Nancy Shaw (Houghton Mifflin)
<u>Shoes from Grandpa</u> - Mem Fox (Scholastic, <u>Literacy Place</u>)

Shared Reading:
<u>Who's in the Shed</u> - Brenda Parkes (Rigby, Big Book)
<u>Mrs. Wish-Washy</u> - Joy Cowley (The Wright Group)
<u>Woosh!</u> - June Melser (The Wright Group)
<u>Oh, A-Hunting We Will Go</u> - (Houghton Mifflin)

Rhymes:
"Baa-Baa, Black Sheep" - Mother Goose
"The Old Women Who Lived in a Shoe" - Mother Goose
"Bobby Shaftoe" - Mother Goose
"My Shadow" - Robert L. Stevenson and illustrated by Ted Rand
   (Putnam)

Song:
"The Sharing Song" - Raffi in <u>Singable Songs for the Very Young</u> (A&M)

Direct Instruction: /sh/

1. Display the digraph <u>sh</u>. Tell the children that you think of it as "the quiet sound" because it is the sound people make when they want others to be quiet. Demonstrate.

2. Ask the children to put their fingers over their lips while making the <u>sh</u> sound.

3. Have the students trace "sh" onto the carpet as they make its sound.

Working With Letters and Sounds

1. Ask the children to make three adjacent squares called *soundboxes* on their chalkboards or papers.

Unit V
Lesson 3

2. Dictate the following words: <u>ship</u>, <u>shop</u>, <u>shut</u>, <u>wish</u>, <u>dish</u>, <u>fish</u>, <u>sash</u>, <u>dash</u>. Ask the children to write the letters that represent the beginning, middle, and final sounds in their squares. Make sure they understand "sh" represents <u>one sound</u>.

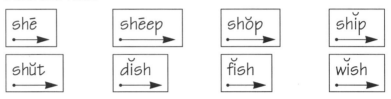

ship   wish

sh	i	p

w	i	sh

Blend, Read and Write

1. Blend and read:

shē	shēep	shŏp	shĭp
shŭt	dĭsh	fĭsh	wĭsh

2. Write: She will make a wish.

Word Construction

1. Ask the children to sort for the following letters (page 351):

s	h	t	p	i	o	w	d	f	e	e

2. Make the following words: <u>sheep</u>, <u>sheet</u>, <u>shop</u>, <u>ship</u>, <u>wish</u>, <u>dish</u>, <u>fish</u>, <u>shot</u>.

Books to Enhance Reading Comprehension, Skill and Language Development

Guided Reading:

<u>Don't Wake the Baby</u> - Pam Neville (Rigby)

<u>She Said</u> - Leya Roberts (Modern Curriculum Press, <u>Ready Readers</u>)

Independent Reading:

Add <u>The Three Little Pigs</u> - Brenda Parkes (Rigby, Big Book) and "Come In, Boo Bear" - David McPhailin in <u>Beginning to Read, Book A</u> (Houghton Mifflin)

Writing Frame:

My mom <u>[likes to swim]</u>.
She <u>[takes me with her]</u>.

Make Your Own Little Books:

<u>A-Hunting We Will Go</u>, pages 161-162. (Book 33)

Letter Cards for Word Construction (page 351)

Word Cards for Sentence Construction (page 352)

Oh-a-hunting we will go
A-hunting we will go
We'll catch a sheep
And put him in a jeep
And then we'll go to
sleep!

8

A-Hunting We Will Go

Name _____

1

Oh-a-hunting we will go
A-hunting we will go
We'll catch an ox
And put him in a box
And then we'll let him go.

6

Oh-a-hunting we will go
A-hunting we will go
We'll catch a fish
And put him in a dish
And then we'll let him go!

3

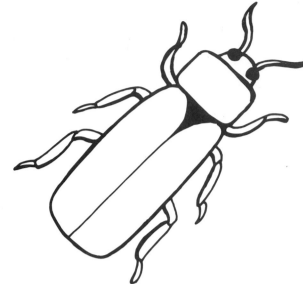

Oh-a-hunting we will go
A-hunting we will go
We'll catch a snail
And put him in a pail
And then we'll let him go.

2

Oh-a-hunting we will go
A-hunting we will go
We'll catch a bug
And put him on a rug
And then we'll let him go

7

Oh-a-hunting we will go
A-hunting we will go
We'll catch a frog
And put him on a log
And then we'll let him go.

4

Oh-a-hunting we will go
A-hunting we will go
We'll catch a dog
And put him in a bog
And then we'll let him go.

5

162
Reproducible

Unit V
Lesson 4

Sight Vocabulary:

- Review <u>do</u>, <u>come</u>, <u>hello</u>, <u>good</u>, <u>ok</u>
- Phonics and Structural Analysis: /ch/; don't

Spelling: much, such, lunch, bunch, chin, fin, cheek, peek

Grammar, Mechanics and Usage:

Possessive (cat's paw)

Developing Phonemic Awareness

Reading Aloud:

<u>Annie, Bea and Chi Chi Dolores</u> - Danna Mauer (Houghton Mifflin)

<u>Chicka Chicka Boom Boom</u> - Bill Martin Jr. (Simon & Schuster)

<u>Chicken Soup with Rice</u> - Maurice Sendak (Harper & Row)

<u>Lunch</u> - Denise Fleming (Holt)

<u>Chatting</u> - Shirley Houghes (Candlewick Press)

<u>Peter's Chair</u> - Ezra Jack Keats (Harper)

<u>Titch</u> - Pat Hutchins (Macmillan)

Shared Reading:

<u>Any Kind of Dog</u> - Lynn Reiser (Harcourt <u>Signatures</u>, Big Book)

<u>Choo Choo</u> - Virginia Lee Burton (Houghton Mifflin)

<u>Good Morning Chick</u> - Mirra Ginsburg in <u>Beginning to Read, Book B</u>
   (Houghton Mifflin <u>Literary Readers</u>)

The Little <u>Engine That Could</u> - Watty Piper (Scholastic)

<u>The Three Little Pigs</u> - Brenda Parkes (Rigby, Big Book)

<u>The Five Chinese Brothers</u> - Claire Huchet Bishop (Putnam)

<u>Chicken Little</u> - Janet Hillman (Rigby, Big Book)

<u>The Chick and the Duckling</u> - Mirra Ginsburg (Houghton Mifflin <u>Invitations
   to Literacy</u>, Big Book) Also in Scholastic's <u>Literacy Place</u>.

Rhymes and Poems:

"March Winds"

   March winds and April showers

   Bring forth May flowers

"Chook Chook" - Mother Goose

Songs:

"The Chimney Sweep Song" (from <u>Mary Poppins</u> video by Walt Disney)

"Rock-A-Motion Choo Choo" - Greg and Steve in <u>We All Live Together,
   Volume 1</u> (Youngheart Records)

163

Direct Instruction: /ch/

1. Show the digraph <u>ch</u> to the children. Explain that the two letters represent <u>one sound</u>.

2. Tell the students that <u>ch</u> reminds you of chocolate chip cookies because "chocolate" and "chip" both begin with <u>ch</u>. Continue to say that <u>ch</u> also reminds you of a <u>choo-choo</u> train. Say "Would you like to eat <u>chocolate chip</u> cookies on a <u>choo-choo</u> train?" Be careful to pronounce "train" distinctly.

3. Show the children how to make a "train" with chairs. Distribute chocolate chip cookies to everyone who can give you a word that begins with "ch." Make sure everyone is successful.

4. Climb aboard your "train" while <u>chomping chocolate chip cookies</u>. The little engineers can say <u>ch-ch-ch</u> as the "train moves."

5. Trace <u>ch</u> onto the carpet while making the sound it represents.

Working With Letters and Sounds

1. Ask the children to draw three adjacent squares called soundboxes on their chalkboards or papers.

2. Dictate the following words: <u>children</u>, <u>chest</u>, <u>rich</u>, <u>catch</u>, <u>match</u>, <u>cheek</u>, <u>chosen</u>, <u>witch</u>. Ask each child to indicate the position of the <u>ch</u> sound by writing the letters in the first or last box. They can also write the first letter of the last sound they hear.

children   witch

| ch | | n | | w | | ch |

Blend, Read and Write

1. Blend and read:

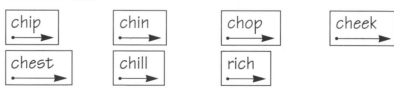

chip   chin   chop   cheek

chest   chill   rich

2. Write: Rich likes to eat chips .

Unit V
Lesson 4

Word Construction

1. Ask the children to sort for the following letters (page 353):

c	h	i	o	p	k	r	s	t	n	a	e	e

2. Make these words: <u>chip</u>, <u>chop</u>, <u>cheek</u>, <u>rich</u>, <u>chest</u>, <u>chin</u>, <u>chat</u>, <u>chap</u>.

Books to Enhance Reading Comprehension, Skill and Language Development

Guided Reading:

<u>Chocolate Chip Cookies</u> - Emily Abbot (Modern Curriculum Press, <u>Ready Readers</u>)

<u>Watch Out!</u> - Jackie Goodyear (Rigby)

Independent Reading:

Add <u>Don't Wake the Baby</u> - Pam Neville (Rigby)

<u>Mrs Wishy-Washy</u> - Joy Cowley (Wright Group)

<u>Who's in the Shed</u> - Brenda Parkes (Rigby, Big Book)

<u>Woosh</u>! - June Mesler (Wright Group)

Writing Frame:

I had a good lunch.

I had_____.

It was_____.

Make Your Own Little Books:

<u>Fox Wants Lunch</u>, pages 166-167. (Book 34)

Letter Cards for Word Construction (page 353)

Word Cards for Sentence Construction (page 354)

"No," said the fox.
"I WANT YOU!"

8

Fox Wants Lunch

Name _____

1

"No," said the fox.

6

"Do you want this apple?" asked the pig.

3

"I want lunch," said the fox to the pig.

2

"Do you want this orange?" asked the pig.

7

 -

"No," said the fox.

4

"Do you want this banana?" asked the pig.

5

167

Unit V
Lesson 5

Sight Vocabulary:

- Review <u>do</u>, <u>come</u>, <u>hello</u>, <u>good</u>, <u>OK</u>
- Phonics and Structural Analysis: /hw/ <u>wh</u> phonogram _en

Spelling: when, Ben, den, hen, Jen, Ken, men, pen, ten; which

Grammar, Mechanics and Usage:

Comma for pausing after a clause (When I play, I play.)

Developing Phonemic Awareness

Read Aloud:

<u>Whistle for Willie</u> - Ezra Jack Keats (Viking)

<u>The Wheeling and Whirling Book</u> - Judy Hindley (Candlewick)

<u>Lentil</u> - Robert McCloskey (Viking)

Shared Reading:

<u>The Wheels on the Bus</u> - Raffi (Crown Books)

Rhymes:

"Little Jumping Joan" - Mother Goose

"Mary Had a Little Lamb" - Mother Goose

"There Was a Little Girl" - Mother Goose

Songs:

"Baby Beluga" - Raffi in <u>Baby Beluga</u> (MCA)

"Wheels on the Bus" - Raffi in <u>Rise and Shine</u> (Troubadour Records, Ltd.)

Direct Instruction: /wh/

1. Show the digraph <u>wh</u>. Tell the children that when you were little, you tried to whistle like Lentil (in <u>Lentil</u> by R. McCloskey, Puffin) but nothing would come out but air (purse your lips together and make the <u>wh</u> sound).

2. Ask children to purse their lips and "blow out" the <u>wh</u> sound.

3. Trace the <u>wh</u> onto the carpet while making its sound.

Working With Letters and Sounds

1. Ask the children to draw three adjacent squares called soundboxes on their chalkboards or papers.

168

Unit V
Lesson 5

2. Dictate the following words: <u>what</u>, <u>when</u>, <u>whistle</u>, <u>whatever</u>, <u>whale</u>, <u>why</u>, <u>which</u>, <u>whisper</u>, <u>wheel</u>. Ask the children to write the letters they hear at the beginning and ending of each word.

wheel

wh		l

whisper

wh		r

Blend, Read and Write

1. Blend and read.

whĭch   whĕn   whĭp   whĭsk   whēel

2. Write: When will he be ten?

Word Construction

1. Ask children to sort for the following letters (page 355):

h	w	n	e	t	m	h	d	p	K	B

2. Make these words: <u>when</u>, <u>den</u>, <u>hen</u>, <u>men</u>, <u>pen</u>, <u>ten</u>, <u>Ken</u>, <u>Ben</u>

Books to Enhance Reading Comprehension, Skill and Language Development

Guided Reading:

<u>Whale Watch</u> - Judy Sperack (Modern Curriculum Press, <u>Ready Readers</u>)

<u>When I Play</u> - Andrea Butler (Rigby)

<u>When It Rains, It Rains</u> - Bill Martin, Jr. (Holt)

Independent Reading:

Add <u>Watch Out</u>! - Jackie Goodyear (Rigby)

<u>Chicka Chicka Boom Boom</u> Bill Martin, Jr. (Simon & Schuster)

<u>Good Morning, Chick</u> - Mirra Ginsburg in <u>Beginning to Read, Book B</u> (Houghton Mifflin, <u>Literary Readers</u>)

Writing Frame:

When I was a baby

I _____.

Make Your Own Little Books:

<u>When I Come, I Come</u>, pages 170-171. (Book 35)

Letter Cards for Word Construction (page 355)

Word Cards for Sentence Construction (page 356)

I say, "Good bye!"

8

When I Come, I Come

Name _____

1

✂ - ✂

When I say hello,
I say hello.

6

When I go, I go.

3

When I come, I come.

2

When I say goodbye . . .

7

When I laugh, I laugh.

4

171
Reproducible

When I cry, I cry.

5

© Fearon Teacher Aids FE7948

Unit V
Lesson 6

Sight Vocabulary:

- Review <u>do</u>, <u>come</u>, <u>hello</u>, <u>good</u>, <u>OK</u>
- Introduce <u>what</u>
- Phonics and Structural Analysis: ŏo (bŏok) phonogram _ook (book); ing (looking)

Spelling: what; look, book, cook, took, shook

Grammar, Mechanics and Usage:

Comma after "no." Review question and answer format

Developing Phonemic Awareness

Read Aloud:

<u>The Important Book</u> - Margaret Wise Brown (Harper)

<u>Look Again!</u> - Tana Hoban (Macmillan)

<u>The Foot Book</u> - Dr. Seuss (Harper)

<u>Zoo-Looking</u> - Mem Fox (Mondo)

Shared Reading:

<u>The Three Little Pigs</u> - Brenda Parkes (Rigby, Big Book)

<u>The Gingerbread Man</u> - Brenda Parkes (Rigby, Big Book)

<u>Who Took the Farmer's Hat</u> - Joan Nodset (Big Book edition with Heath Kindergarten Program)

Rhyme:

"Chook, Chook, Chook" - Mother Goose

Song:

"Biscuits in the Oven" - Raffi in <u>Baby Beluga</u> (MCA)

Direct Instruction: /ŏo/ _ŏok

1. Explain to the children that sometimes when two <u>o's</u> are together, they stand for the sound you hear in the middle of <u>look</u>. Say "The word <u>look</u> is easy to remember because two eyes 'look' at <u>you</u> when <u>you</u> look at the word."

2. Challenge the children to learn to spell the word <u>look</u>. Tell them to:

1. Copy the word
2. Cover the word.
3. Try to write the word without looking.
4. Try again.

Working With Letters and Sounds

1. Ask the children to draw three adjacent squares called *soundboxes* on their chalkboards or papers.

2. Dictate the following words: <u>look</u>, <u>book</u>, <u>cook</u>, <u>took</u>, <u>hook</u>, <u>rook</u>, <u>shook</u>, <u>nook</u>. Have the students write the letters that represent the beginning, middle and final sounds.

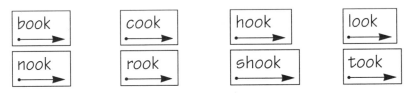

cook   shook   book

| c | oo | k |

| sh | oo | k |

| b | oo | k |

Blend, Read and Write

1. Blend and read:

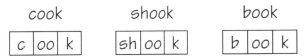

book   cook   hook   look

nook   rook   shook   took

2. Write: Will you look at this book?

Word Construction

1. Ask the children to sort for the following letters (page 357):

| l | k | t | <u>b</u> | r | c | n | h | s | h | o | o |

2. Make these words: <u>look</u>, <u>book</u>, <u>cook</u>, <u>took</u>, <u>shook</u>, <u>nook</u>, <u>rook</u>, <u>hook</u>.

Unit V
Lesson 6

Tip:

Hide something in a lunch bag. Write clues on the outside of the bag. Children read clues; other children guess what's inside the bag.

Books to Enhance Reading Comprehension, Skill and Language Development

Guided Reading:

Look Closer - Claudia Logan (Modern Curriculum Press, Ready Readers)

My Book - Ron Maris (Viking Penguin)

What Goes in the Bathtub? - Pam Neville (Rigby)

Independent Reading:

Add When I Play - Andrea Butler (Rigby) and other books introduced to the class.

Writing Frame:

What Is It?

It _____.

It _____.

It _____.

What is it?

Make Your Own Little Books:

What Can You See? pages 175-176. (Book 36)

Letter Cards for Word Construction (page 357)

Word Cards for Sentence Construction (page 358)

I see the **teacher**
looking at me!

8

What Can You See?

Name _____

1

Look, look.
What can you see?

6

I see a boy
looking at me.

3

Look, look.
What can you see?

2

I see a fish looking at me.

7

Look, look.
What can you see?

4

176
Reproducible

I see a girl looking at me.

5

Sight Vocabulary:

- ■ Review do, come, hello, good, OK, what
- ■ Introduce <u>my</u>
- ■ Phonics and Structural Analysis: /ā/ a-e phonograms _ame and _ake

Spelling: came, game, name, same; bake, cake, lake, make, take, wake.

Grammar, Mechanics and Usage:

Review punctuation for a statement ("telling sentence"); questions

Developing Phonemic Awareness

Read Aloud:

<u>The Cake That Mack Ate</u> - Rose Robart (Little, Brown)

Shared Reading:

<u>The Little Red Hen</u> - Brenda Parkes (Rigby, Big Book)

Rhyme:

"Pat-a-Cake" - Mother Goose

Song:

"Shake My Sillies Out" - Raffi in <u>More Singable Songs</u> (A&M)

Direct Instruction: /ā/ a-e

1. Tell the children that they are about to play a guessing game. Explain that you will write two lists of words on the board because they demonstrate a rule about reading words. You want them to try to figure out what the rule is. Write these words while the children watch:

can	cane
rat	rate
back	bake
lack	lake

2. Give clues until the children observe that the words on the right end with "e." Help them to realize that this "e" (e marker or "magic e") "signals" the "a" to "say its own name - ā." Use a pocket chart to classify words.

Unit V
Lesson 7

3. Give children word cards (pages 180-181) with short and long "a" sounds. Reproduce cards on construction paper. Have children cut out the cards on the dotted lines. Let them classify according to the "e marker" rule.

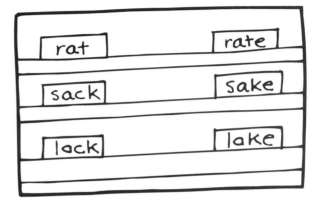

Working With Letters and Sounds

1. Ask the children to draw three adjacent squares called *soundboxes* on their chalkboards or papers.

2. Dictate the following words: <u>game</u>, <u>same</u>, <u>take</u>, <u>wake</u>, <u>make</u>, <u>came</u>, <u>shame</u>, <u>bake</u>. Direct the children to write the beginning, medial and final sounds in their squares. Direct them to draw a broken line through the "e" to show that it does not represent a sound of its own.

c	ā	me̸

3. Ask "How many <u>sounds</u> can you hear in <u>came</u>? How many letters does it have?"

Blend, Read and Write

1. Blend and read:

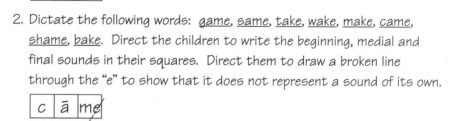

Word Construction

1. Ask the children to sort for the following letters (page 359):

c	a	k	e	b	s	m	t	f

2. Make these words: <u>cake</u>, <u>bake</u>, <u>sake</u>, <u>make</u>, <u>take</u>, <u>fake</u>, <u>came</u>, <u>same</u>, <u>tame</u>, <u>fame</u>.

Unit V
Lesson 7

Books to Enhance Reading Comprehension, Skill and Language Development

Guided Reading:
The Farm - Claudia Logan (Modern Curriculum Press, Ready Readers)
"The Hat" - Laurene Krasy Brown in Beginning to Read, Book A
    (Houghton Mifflin, Literary Readers)
Have You Seen My Cat? - Eric Carle (Scholastic Literacy Place)
The Pet Parade - Andrea Butler (Rigby)
What Can You Make? - Claudia Logan (Modern Curriculum Press, Ready
    Readers)

Writing Frame:
I can make _____.
First_____.
Then _____.

Make Your Own Little Books:
What Do You Want? pages 182-183. (Book 37)

Letter Cards for Word Construction (page 359)

Word Cards for Sentence Construction (page 360)

Evaluation: Unit V

Directions:
1. Ask each child to read the word lists and the sentences.

List A	List B
my	put
come	what
do	here
they	good
want	hello
OK	have
don't	make

Do they want to come?

I don't want to make a cake.

OK, I'll go to see the dog.

2. Dictate the following sentence: Do you want to make a cake?

Directions:

Cut on dotted lines. Classify according to sounds of vowels.

rat	rate
can	cane
back	bake
Mack	make

180

lack	lake
sack	sake
tack	take
Jack	Jake

Reproducible

What Do You Want?

I love you, too!

8

Name _____

1

What?

6

Do you want Mom?

3

What do you want?
Do you want a bottle?

2

Do you want me?

7

 -

Do you want Dad?

4

183

What do you want?

5

Unit VI

Target Word
Recognition Skills:

ay (pay) o-e (home) ōw (show)
ow (now) i-e (kite) _y (fly)
ed (want<u>ed</u>, look<u>ed</u>, learn<u>ed</u>)
kn (know) ai (tail)
ea (eat) ew (grew)
<u>one</u>, <u>know</u>, <u>some</u>, <u>more</u>, <u>your</u>,
<u>goes</u>, <u>was</u>, <u>or</u>, <u>other</u>, <u>been</u>,
<u>would</u>, <u>mother</u>, <u>two</u>

Unit VI Lesson 1

Sight Vocabulary:

- Introduce *goes*
- Phonics and Structural Analysis: /ē/ ea; phonogram _eat

Spelling: eat, beat, heat, meat, neat, seat, wheat, each

Grammar, Mechanics and Usage:
Introduce italics and bold print for emphasis, comma in a series

Developing Phonemic Awareness

Read Aloud:
Early Morning in the Barn - Nancy Tafuri (Greenwillow)
Sheep Out to Eat - Nancy Shaw (Houghton Mifflin)

Shared Reading:
Across the Stream - Mirra Ginsburg (Scholastic Literacy Place, Big Book)
Chicken Little - Janet Hillman (Rigby, Big Book)

Rhymes:
"Little Miss Muffet" - Mother Goose
"Tom, Tom, the Piper's Son" - Mother Goose

Songs:
"Found a Peanut" - Pamela Conn Beall in Wee Sing Silly Songs (Price Stern Sloan)
"Apples and Bananas" - Raffi in One Light, One Sun (MCA)

Direct Instruction: /ē/ ea

1. Remind children that they have learned one spelling for the ē sound: ee; today they will learn another spelling: ea. This is a good time to mention the inconsistencies in the English language, as well as homonyms.

2. Let the children roam around the room with their clipboards. Challenge them to write down as many ee and ea words as they can find. Encourage children to work together.

3. Ask the children to help you make charts showing the words they have discovered. Classify according to spelling.

Working With Letters and Sounds

1. Show children how to make three adjacent squares called *soundboxes* on their chalkboards or papers.

Unit VI
Lesson 1

Tip:
Introduce the child to homonyms within the context of instruction. (meet, meat)

2. Dictate the following words: <u>beat</u>, <u>heat</u>, <u>meat</u>, <u>neat</u>, <u>seat</u>, <u>wheat</u>, <u>feat</u>, <u>peat</u>.

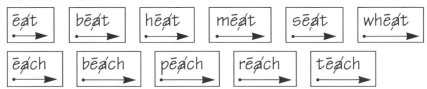

wheat | seat

| wh | ea | t |

| s | ea | t |

Blend, Read and Write

1. Blend and read:

| ēat → | bēat → | hēat → | mēat → | sēat → | whēat → |

| ēach → | bēach → | pēach → | rēach → | tēach → |

2. Write: I like to eat meat.

Word Construction

1. Ask the children to sort for the following letters (page 361):

| b | t | m | n | f | s | h | w | e | a |

2. Make these words: <u>beat</u>, <u>meat</u>, <u>eat</u>, <u>wheat</u>, <u>neat</u>, <u>seat</u>, <u>heat</u>, <u>feat</u>.

Books to Enhance Reading Comprehension, Skill and Language Development

Guided Reading:

<u>Dee and Me</u> - Lois Bick (Modern Curriculum Press, <u>Ready Readers</u>)
"Cat Goes Fiddle-i-Fee" - Paul Galdone in <u>Beginning to Read, Book B</u>
    (Houghton Mifflin, <u>Literary Readers</u>)

Independent Reading:

Add <u>The Pet Parade</u> - Andrea Butler (Rigby)

Activity for Home or School

Have the children trace over the word <u>goes</u> with crayon or glue. Take home to practice.

Writing Frame:

I like to eat _____, _____ and
_____. I don't like _____.

Make Your Own Little Books:

<u>The Little Red Hen</u>, pages 187-188. (Book 38)

Letter Cards for Word Construction (page 361)

Word Cards for Sentence Construction (page 362)

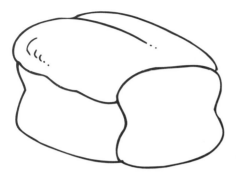

"And I will eat it myself, too," said the little red hen. And she did.

8

The Little Red Hen

Traditional

Name _____

1

"Who will help me bake the bread?" asked the little red hen.

6

"Not I," said the cat.
"Not I," said the dog.
"Not I," said the duck.
"Then I will do it myself," said the little red hen. And she did.

3

"Who will help me plant the wheat?" asked the little red hen.

2

"Not I," said the cat.
"Not I," said the dog.
"Not I," said the duck.
"Then I will do it myself," said the little red hen.
And she did.

7

"Who will help me cut the wheat?" asked the little red hen.

4

188
Reproducible

"Not I," said the cat.
"Not I," said the dog.
"Not I," said the duck.
"Then I will do it myself," said the little red hen.
And she did.

5

Sight Vocabulary:

- Review <u>goes</u>
- Introduce <u>was</u>
- Phonics and Structural Analysis: /ā/ (ay)
- Phonogram _ay; compound words

Spelling: day, hay, lay, may, pay, say, stay, way, play, today

Grammar, Mechanics and Usage:
Use of the comma after a pause in a sentence

Developing Phonemic Awareness

Read Aloud:
<u>Today Is Monday</u> - Eric Carle (Philomel)

Shared Reading:
<u>What Will the Weather Be Like Today?</u> - Paul Rogers (Greenwillow)

Rhymes:
"Rain, Rain, Go Away" - Mother Goose
<u>Time for a Number Rhymes</u> - (Rigby, Big Book)
<u>Time for a Rhyme</u> - (Rigby, Big Book)
<u>Gobble, Gobble, Gulp Gulp</u> - (Rigby, Big Book)

Song:
"Down By the Bay" - Raffi in <u>Singable Songs for the Very Young</u> (A&M)

Direct Instruction: /ā/ _ay

1. Tell the children that many "little words" that end with the sound <u>ā</u> are spelled <u>ay</u> as in <u>day</u>, <u>may</u>, <u>say</u>.

2. Look up at the alphabet and say "If I put a 'b' in front of 'ay,' I get <u>bay</u>." Give the children a few minutes to come up with other words by substituting other consonants.

3. Write the children's responses on the board. Accept nonsense responses, but challenge the children to find the words "that we use when we talk, read or write."

Working With Letters and Sounds

1. Ask the children to draw <u>two</u> adjacent squares called *soundboxes* on their chalkboards or papers.

Unit VI
Lesson 2

2. Dictate the following words: <u>may</u>, <u>bay</u>, <u>day</u>, <u>hay</u>, <u>lay</u>, <u>pay</u>, <u>ray</u>, <u>say</u>. Ask the children to write the letters that represent the sounds in the squares.

say

s	ay

Blend, Read and Write

1. Blend and read:

2. Write: We will go this way.

Word Construction

1. Ask the children to sort for the following letters (page 363):

m	s	d	l	w	p	h	a	y

2. Make these words: <u>may</u>, <u>day</u>, <u>say</u>, <u>lay</u>, <u>way</u>, <u>pay</u>, <u>play</u>, <u>hay</u>.

Books to Enhance Reading Comprehension, Skill and Language Development

Guided Reading:

<u>Nanny Goat's Nap</u> - Ashley Dennis (Modern Curriculum Press, <u>Ready Readers</u>)

<u>When I Was Sick</u> - Janet Hillman (Rigby)

Independent Reading:

Add "Cat Goes Fiddle-i-Fee" - Paul Galdone in <u>Beginning to Read, Book B</u> (Houghton Mifflin, <u>Literary Readers</u>)

Activity for Home or School

Make flip books to practice the phonogram "_ay." Write the word <u>may</u> on an index card. On pieces of paper large enough to cover the first letter write <u>s</u>, <u>d</u>, <u>l</u>, <u>w</u>, <u>p</u>, <u>h</u>. Staple these papers together to make flip books.

Make Your Own Little Books:

<u>Playtime</u>, pages 191-192. (Book 39)

Letter Cards for Word Construction (page 363)

Word Cards for Sentence Construction (page 364)

They do **not** like to stop!

8

Playtime

Name _____

1

 ✂ --- ✂

They like to run.

6

She plays with Jess.
They like to play baseball.

3 © Fearon Teacher Aids FE7948

When Jen plays,
she goes to the park.

2

They like to swing.

7

They like to play
in the sandbox.

4

They like to ride on the
seesaw. Jess goes up.
Jen goes down.

5

Unit VI
Lesson 3

Sight Vocabulary:

- Review _goes_
- Introduce _some_
- Phonics and Structural Analysis: compound words

Spelling: some, goes

Grammar, Mechanics and Usage:

Comma in a series

Developing Phonemic Awareness

Read Aloud:

Someday - Charlotte Zolotow (Harper)

The Shoemaker and the Elves - Freya Littledale (Scholastic)

Shared Reading:

Jack in the Beanstalk - Brenda Parkes (Rigby, Big Book)

Moonbear's Books - Frank Asch (Houghton Mifflin, Invitations to Literacy, Big Book)

Rhymes:

"Little Miss Muffet" - Mother Goose

"Pease Porridge Hot" - Mother Goose

Song:

"Pop Goes the Weasel" in Jane Yolen's Mother Goose Songbook (Boyds Mills Press)

Direct Instruction: Compound Words

1. Draw the children's attention to the title Someday. Tell them that the word is actually made up of two other words: some and day. Therefore, it is called a compound word. "Compound" means "two or more."

2. Tell the children that you are going to read to them from a Big Book that they have heard before, but this time you would like them to be on the lookout for compound words. Ask them to raise their hands every time you come to a compound word. A number of them can be found in Rigby Big Books.

Unit VI
Lesson 3

Books to Enhance Reading Comprehension, Skill and Language Development

Guided Reading:
Jim's Visit to Kim - Julius Alperon (Modern Curriculum Press, Ready Readers)

Sunrise - Ron Bacon (Rigby)

Independent Reading:
Add Down By the Bay - Raffi (Crown Books)

When I Was Sick - Janet Hillman (Rigby)

Activity for Home or School: Compound Words

1. Ask the children to help you make a "compound word" game. Show the children how to make compound word puzzle strips. Some examples of compound word cards can be found on page 365.

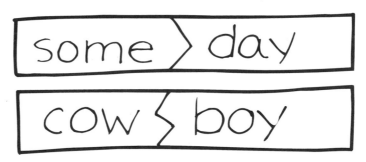

2. Let the children place their puzzles into a decorated box for independent practice.

Writing Frame:
Someday I _____

_____.

Make Your Own Little Books:
Someday, pages 195-196. (Book 40)

Compound Word Cards for Activity for Home or School (page 365)

Word Cards for Sentence Construction (page 366)

"Just like you."

8

Someday

Name _____

1

✂ - ✂

"Someday I want to be a ballerina," said Pam.

6

"Someday I want to be a teacher," said Brad.

3

"Someday I want
to be an airplane
pilot," said Cris.

2

"Someday I want to be a
grandfather," said Kev.

7

"Someday I want to be
a doctor," said Ed.

4

"Someday I want to be
a trucker," said Don.

5

Sight Vocabulary:

- Review <u>more</u>, <u>one</u>
- Introduce <u>two</u>
- Phonics and Structural Analysis: /ôr/

Spelling: or, for, born, torn, worn, one, more

Grammar, Mechanics and Usage: A complete sentence

Developing Phonemic Awareness

Read Aloud:

<u>Norma Jean, Jumping Bean</u> - Joanna Cole (Random House)

<u>A Kiss For Little Bear</u> - Else Minarid (Harper)

<u>More, More, More, Said the Baby</u> - Vera Williams (Scholastic)

Shared Reading:

<u>The Enormous Watermelon</u> - Brenda Parkes (Rigby, Big Book)

<u>One More Thing, Dad</u> - Susan L. Thompson (Houghton Mifflin, <u>Literary Readers, Book 1</u>)

Rhymes and Poems:

<u>Time for Rhyme</u> - (Rigby, Big Book)

"Little Boy Blue" - Mother Goose

Songs:

"Mary Wore Her Red Dress" - Raffi in <u>Everything Grows</u> (MCA)

"Jimmy Crack Corn" - Greg and Steve in <u>Kidding Around With Greg and Steve</u> (Youngheart Records)

"De Colores" - Raffi in <u>One Light, One Sun</u> (MCA)

Direct Instruction: /ôr/

Show the word <u>or</u>. Tell the children that this is the word <u>or</u> - "I like this <u>or</u> that." Explain that when these two letters are part of a word, it also stands for the sound "or." Give examples: <u>corn</u>, <u>torn</u>, <u>horn</u>.

Working With Letters and Sounds

1. Ask children to draw three adjacent squares called soundboxes on their chalkboards or papers.

Unit VI
Lesson 4

2. Dictate the following words: <u>corn</u>, <u>torn</u>, <u>born</u>, <u>worn</u>, <u>horn</u>, <u>short</u>, <u>north</u>, <u>fort</u>.

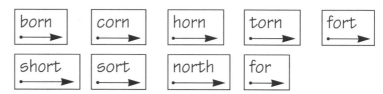

Blend, Read and Write

1. Blend and read:

| born → | corn → | horn → | torn → | fort → |

| short → | sort → | north → | for → |

2. Write: Tom has corn for you.

Word Construction

1. Ask the children to sort for the following letters (page 367):

| f | t | <u>c</u> | <u>n</u> | h | <u>b</u> | o | r |

2. Make these words: <u>for</u>, <u>corn</u>, <u>horn</u>, <u>thorn</u>, <u>north</u>, <u>torn</u>, <u>born</u>, <u>fort</u>.

Books to Enhance Reading Comprehension, Skill and Language Development

Guided Reading:

<u>A Sea Star</u> - Anne Miranda (Modern Curriculum Press, <u>Ready Readers</u>)

<u>Sharing</u> - Andrea Butler (Rigby)

Independent Reading:

Add <u>A Scrumptious Sundae</u>

Writing Frame:

I am _____.
I was born_____.
My _____.
I like to _____.

Make Your Own Little Books:

<u>Five Dollars</u>, pages 199-200. (Book 41)

Letters Cards for Word Construction (page 367)

Word Cards for Sentence Construction (page 368)

I can go get
that red horn.

8

Five Dollars

Name _____

1

Grandma gave
me one more.
That's five dollars.

6

Dad gave me
one more.
That's two dollars.

3

I had a dollar.

2

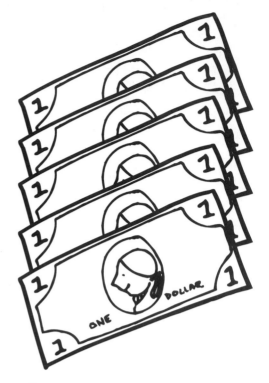

One, two, three,
four, five dollars!

7

Mom gave me
one more.
That's three dollars.

4

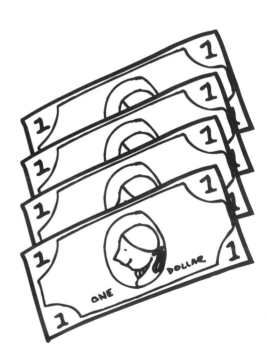

Grandpa gave
me one more.
That's four dollars.

5

Sight Vocabulary:

- Review <u>more</u>, <u>one</u>
- Introduce <u>know</u>
- Phonics and Structural Analysis: /ou/ ow (how) /ō/ ow (crow)

Spelling: cow, how, now, brown, town, down

Grammar, Mechanics and Usage:
Sentence as a command

Developing Phonemic Awareness

Reading Aloud:

<u>Ask Mr. Bear</u> - Marjorie Flack (Macmillan)

<u>Look</u> - Michael Grejniec (North-South Books)

<u>Papa, Please Get the Moon for Me</u> - Eric Carle (Scholastic)

<u>The Snowy Day</u> - Ezra Jack Keats (Viking) Also, included in Scholastic's <u>Literacy Place</u>.

<u>Owen</u> - Kevin Henkes (Greenwillow)

Shared Reading:

<u>The Three Little Pigs</u> - Brenda Parkes (Rigby, Big Book)

<u>Jack and the Beanstalk</u> - Brenda Parkes (Rigby, Big Book)

Rhymes:

"Hey! Diddle, Diddle!" - Mother Goose

"Mary Had a Little Lamb" in <u>Jane Yolen's Mother Goose Songbook</u> (Boyds Mills Press)

Songs:

"Do Your Ears Hang Low?" - <u>Wee Sing Silly Songs</u> (Price Stern Sloan)

"Who Did Swallow Jonah?" - <u>Wee Sing Silly Songs</u> (Price Stern Sloan)

"I Know an Old Lady" - <u>If You're Happy and You Know It: Eighteen Story Songs Set to Pictures</u> (Greenwillow)

Direct Instruction: ōw (grow) ow (now)

1. Tell the children you have a puzzle for them. Tell them that there are two words in English that are spelled the same way - <u>bow</u> and <u>bow</u> (write both words on the board), but have completely different meanings and pronunciations. One means a <u>bow</u> in your hair and one is a <u>bow</u> (bow for the children). Say, "Now here is the puzzle. If you saw this word in a book, how would you know how to pronounce it?"

Unit VI
Lesson 5

2. Hopefully, someone will guess "the other words in the sentence." If not, give more clues. Then write the following sentence on the board:

> The man will <u>bow</u> to the king.
> The girl had a <u>bow</u> in her hair.

Ask the children to read these sentences silently. Call on volunteers to read them aloud.

3. On a pocket chart have the students classify sentences with <u>ow</u> words.

ow cow	ow know
Please come <u>now</u>.	I <u>know</u> how to do it.
Will you <u>bow</u> to him?	She has a red <u>bow</u>.
Come <u>down</u> with me.	He has a <u>bowl</u> of milk.
The <u>cow</u> will give milk.	The <u>scarecrow</u> scares me.

Working With Letters and Sounds

1. Ask children to draw three adjacent squares called soundboxes on their chalkboards or papers.

2. Dictate the following words: <u>town</u>, <u>gown</u>, <u>down</u>.

down

d	ow	n

3. Make "soundboxes" with <u>two</u> squares.

4. Dictate <u>now</u>, <u>how</u>, <u>bow</u>, <u>cow</u>.

now

n	ow

202

Unit VI
Lesson 5

Blend, Read and Write

1. Blend and read:

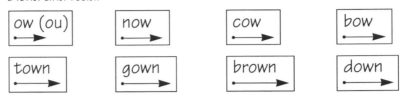

| ow (ou) | now | cow | bow |
| town | gown | brown | down |

2. Write: Now I'll get the brown cow.

Word Construction

1. Ask the children to sort for the following letters (page 369):

n c b d t r f h o w

2. Make these words: now, cow, bow, how, town, brown, down, frown

Books to Enhance Reading Comprehension, Skill and Language Development

Guided Reading:

Can a Cow Hop? - Carly Easton (Modern Curriculum Press, Ready Readers)

The Scarecrow - Ron Bacon (Rigby)

Squirrels - Gale Clifford (Modern Curriculum Press, Ready Readers)

Independent Reading:

Add Sharing - Andrea Butler (Rigby)

Activity for Home or School

Write the word know on a card. Trace with crayon or glue. Take home to practice.

Writing Frame:

I know how to _____.

First I_____.

Then I _____.

Make Your Own Little Books:

A Clay Cow, pages 204-205. (Book 42)

Letter Cards for Word Construction (page 369)

Word Cards for Sentence Construction (page 370)

Tip:

Here's an amusing way to help children remember that kn represents the /n/ sound:
Tell the children that you had an interesting experience that you would like to share with them. (Pronounce the "k" sound in each word.) Say "I went to K - notts Berry Farm and do you k - now what happened to me? I fell off a ride and hurt my k - nee." The children will correct you and laugh, but most of all, they'll never forget know and the kn sound.

(Idea courtesy of Tammy McQuade, teacher at Frank E. Woodruff School in Bellflower, CA.)

Good job!

8

A Clay Cow

1

 -

Then you paint it.

6

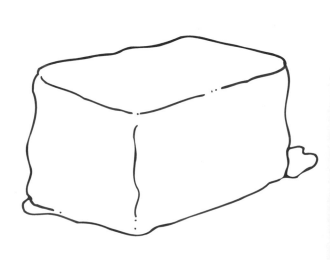

First you get some clay.

3

204
Reproducible

© Fearon Teacher Aids FE7948

I want to make a
cow out of clay.
I know how to do it.

2

Then you let it stay here
for one more day.

7

Then you make the cow.

4

Then you put it in
the sun for a day.

5

205
Reproducible

Unit VI
Lesson 6

Sight Vocabulary:

■ Review <u>more</u>, <u>one</u>, <u>know</u>
■ Phonics and Structural Analysis: /ō/ o-e (home)

Spelling: hope, rope, bone, cone, joke, broke, woke, hole, pole, home

Grammar, Mechanics and Usage: Review conventions

Developing Phonemic Awareness

Read Aloud:

<u>Stone Soup</u> - Marcia Brown (Scribner)

Shared Reading:

"Over in the Meadow" - Ezra Jack Keats (<u>Beginning to Read, Book B</u>, Houghton Mifflin)

Rhymes:

"Little Bo-Peep" - Mother Goose
"Jack and Jill" - Mother Goose

Songs:

"There's a Hole in the Bucket" in <u>Wee Sing Silly Songs</u> (Price Stern Sloan) (Included in Scholastic's <u>Literacy Place</u>)
"Apples and Bananas" - Raffi in <u>One Light One Sun</u> (MCA)

Direct Instruction: /ō/ o-e

1. Remind the children of the word <u>make</u>. Say, "Remember, the 'a' stands for its long sound because there is an 'e' at the end, but the 'e' does not stand for a sound of its own. Some people say that it is 'silent'."

   Continue: "Look at the word <u>home</u>. The 'o' stands for its long sound because there is the 'e' at the end. The 'e' signals the 'o' to make its long sound."

   hōme

2. Give other examples (<u>bone</u>, <u>rope</u>, <u>tone</u>, <u>hope</u>).

Working With Letters and Sounds

1. Ask children to draw three adjacent squares called soundboxes on their chalkboards or papers.

Unit VI
Lesson 6

Dictate the following words: <u>home</u>, <u>vote</u>, <u>cone</u>, <u>tone</u>, <u>bone</u>, <u>note</u>, <u>hope</u>, <u>rode</u>

rode

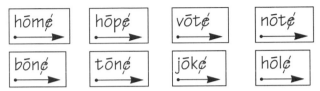

r	o	dé

Blend, Read and Write

1. Blend and read:

hōmé →	hōpé →	vōté →	nōté →

bōné →	tōné →	jōké →	hōlé →

2. Write: I hope we go home.

Word Construction

1. Ask the children to sort for the following letters (page 371):

h	o	e	p	v	l	m	n	t

2. Make these words: <u>hole</u>, <u>home</u>, <u>hope</u>, <u>vote</u>, <u>note</u>, <u>mole</u>, <u>pole</u>, <u>tone</u>.

Books to Enhance Reading Comprehension, Skill and Language Development

Guided Reading:

<u>The Ball Game</u> - Sue Donovan (Rigby)

<u>Sparky's Bone</u> - Claire Daniel (Modern Curriculum Press, <u>Ready Readers</u>)

<u>When Bob Woke Up Late</u> - Robin Bloksberg (Modern Curriculum Press, <u>Ready Readers</u>)

Independent Reading:

Add <u>The Scarecrow</u> - Ron Bacon (Rigby)

Writing Frame:
My Home

My home is _____.

It is _____.

It _____.

I _____.

Make Your Own Little Books:

<u>Dan</u>, pages 208-209. (Book 43)

Letter Cards for Word Construction (page 371)

Word Cards for Sentence Construction (page 372)

> **Tip:**
> Children can write about their real home, or draw their "dream home" before writing about it.

Dan said, "I like it here. I don't want to go home."

8

Dan

Name _____

1

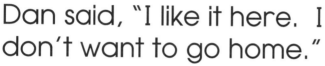

The teacher said, "Don't be sad. Here is a red balloon."

6

The policeman said, "Don't be sad. Here is some ice cream."

3

Dan said, "I am lost. I do not know how to get home." He was very sad.

2

Mom said, "Dan, here I am! We can go home."

7

The firefighter said, "Don't be sad. Here is a lollipop."

4

Reproducible

The doctor said, "Don't be sad. Here is some gum."

5

Unit VI
Lesson 7

Sight Vocabulary:

- Review <u>more</u>, <u>one</u>, <u>know</u>
- Introduce <u>other</u>, <u>been</u>
- Phonics and Structural Analysis: /ā/ ai; it's, can't

Spelling: rain, main, laid, paid, other

Grammar, Mechanics and Usage:

speech marks, exclamation point, emphasis

Developing Phonemic Awareness

Read Aloud:

<u>Bringing The Rain to Kapiti Plain</u> - Verna Aardema (Scholastic)

Rhymes:

"Jack and Jill" - Mother Goose

"Mary Mary Quite Contrary" - Mother Goose

"Rain, Rain, Go Away" - Mother Goose

Songs:

"I've been Working On the Railroad" - Alan and Lea Daniel (Wright Group, Big Book)

Direct Instruction: /ā/ ai

1. Tell the children that <u>ai</u> stands for the ā sound as in <u>rain</u>.

2. Write the following words on a chart or whiteboard. Use blue for the consonants and red for <u>ai</u>.

r<u>ai</u>n   m<u>ai</u>n   tr<u>ai</u>n

Practice reading the words.

Working With Letters and Sounds

1. Ask children to draw three adjacent squares called soundboxes on their chalkboards or papers.

2. Dictate these words: <u>rain</u>, <u>main</u>, <u>pain</u>, <u>laid</u>, <u>paid</u>, <u>pail</u>, <u>mail</u>, <u>tail</u>.

rain

r	ai	n

Unit VI
Lesson 7

Blend, Read and Write

1. Blend and read:

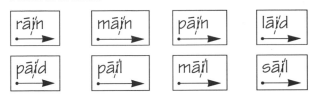

rāin   māin   pāin   lāid
pāid   pāil   māil   sāil

2. Write: I will get the mail.

Word Construction

1. Ask the children to sort for the following letters (page 373):

r   n   m   p   b   r   s   t   d   a   i

2. Make the following words: rain, main, pain, brain, stain, paid, maid, raid.

Books to Enhance Reading Comprehension, Skill and Language Development

Guided Reading:

"A Good Home" - Laurene Krasny Brown (Beginning to Read, Book B, Houghton Mifflin, Literary Readers)

In the Rain - Rebecca Haber (Modern Curriculum Press, Ready Readers)

Activity for Home or School

Write the word other on an index card. Trace over with crayon or glue. Take home to practice.

Writing Frame:

The Rain

One time _____.

I _____.

Make Your Own Little Books:

The Rain, pages 212-213. (Book 44)

Letter Cards for Word Construction (page 373)

Word Cards for Sentence Construction (page 374)

The Rain

get wet!

8

Name _____

1

✂ - ✂

I love to be in the rain.

6

I love to wear
my raincoat.

3

I love the rain!

2

It is so much fun to . . .

7

I love to wear my boots.

4

213
Reproducible

I love to put up
my umbrella.

5

Unit VI
Lesson 8

Sight Vocabulary:

- Review <u>more</u>, <u>one</u>, <u>know</u>
- Introduce <u>your</u>
- Phonics and Structural Analysis: /ī/ -y

Spelling: by, my, fly, sky, try, why

Grammar, Mechanics and Usage: Review conventions.

Developing Phonemic Awareness

Read Aloud:

<u>Is Your Mama a Llama?</u> - D. Guarina (Scholastic, Big Book)

<u>Have You Seen My Cat?</u> - Eric Carle (Scholastic)

<u>Each Peach Pear Plum</u> - Janet and Allan Ahlberg (Puffin)

Shared Reading:

<u>My River</u> - Shari Halpern (Houghton Mifflin, <u>Invitations to Literacy</u>, Big Book)

<u>Who Will Be My Mother?</u> - Joy Cowley (Wright Group, Big Book)

Rhymes:

"Bye Bye Baby Bunting" - Mother Goose

"Twinkle, Twinkle, Little Star" - Mother Goose

Songs:

"There Was An Old Lady Who Swallowed a Fly" - <u>If You're Happy and You Know It: Eighteen Story Songs Set to Pictures</u> (Greenwillow)

"Let's Go Fly a Kite" (from <u>Mary Poppins</u> video)

"Down by the Bay" - Raffi in <u>Singable Songs for the Very Young</u> (A&M)

Direct Instruction: /ī/ -y

1. Remind the children of the names of the vowels: "a, e, i, o, u and sometimes <u>y</u> and sometimes <u>w</u>." Tell them that in the word "fly" the "y" acts as a vowel sound. Explain that when "y" comes at the <u>end</u> of a short word, it usually stands for the ī sound.

2. Give examples: <u>by</u>, <u>my</u>, <u>fly</u>, <u>try</u>, <u>sky</u>, <u>why</u>

Working With Letters and Sounds

1. Ask the children to draw three adjacent squares called soundboxes on their chalkboards or papers.

Tip:

Remember that the words <u>why</u> and <u>shy</u> have only two phonemes.

214

2. Dictate the following words: <u>sky</u>, <u>fly</u>, <u>try</u>, <u>sty</u>, <u>sly</u>, <u>fry</u>, <u>cry</u>, <u>dry</u>

fly

f	l	y

Blend, Read and Write

1. Blend and read:

by →	my →	why →	shy →	try →	cry →	dry →	fry →

2. Write: Why don't you try it?

Word Construction

1. Ask the children to sort for the following letters (page 375):

y	m	t	r	f	l	<u>d</u>	w	<u>s</u>	h

2. Make the following words: <u>my</u>, <u>by</u>, <u>why</u>, <u>shy</u>, <u>try</u>, <u>fry</u>, <u>fly</u>, <u>dry</u>.

Books to Enhance Reading Comprehension, Skill and Language Development

Guided Reading:

<u>Bet You Can't</u> - Penny Dale (Scholastic, <u>Literacy Place</u>)

<u>I Spy</u> - Lucy Lawrence (Rigby)

<u>My Lost Top</u> - Diane Engles (Modern Curriculum Press, <u>Ready Readers</u>)

Independent Reading:

Add "A Good Home" - Laurene Krasny Brown (<u>Beginning to Read, Book B</u>, Houghton Mifflin, <u>Literary Readers</u>)

Activity for Home or School

Write the word <u>your</u> on an index card. Trace the word with crayon or glue. Take it home to practice.

Writing Frame:

"My Kite"

I made _____.

I _____.

It was_____.

Make Your Own Little Books:

<u>A Gift from Dad</u>, pages 216-217. (Book 45)

Letter Cards for Word Construction (page 375)

Word Cards for Sentence Construction (page 376)

Tip:
Have each child make a kite. Take it out to fly before writing about the experience.

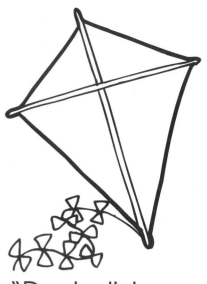

"Dad, did you
get my kite?"
"Yes, I did."
"Thanks, Dad.
Let's go fly it."

8

A Gift from Dad

Name _____

1

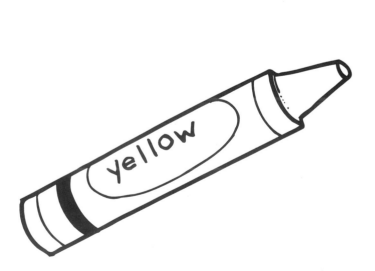

"No," said Dad.
"It is yellow."

6

"Thanks, Dad. What
is it?" asked Jill.

3

Dad said, "Jill, I have a gift for you."

2

"Can it fly?" asked Jill.
"Yes, it can fly," said Dad.

7

"What do you think it is?"

4

"Is it red?" asked Jill.

5

Unit VI
Lesson 9

Sight Vocabulary:

- Review <u>more</u>, <u>one</u>, <u>know</u>, <u>your</u>
- Phonics: /oo/ grew

Spelling: new, blew, chew, grew, stew, flew, drew, crew

Grammar, Mechanics and Usage

Developing Phonemic Awareness

Read Aloud:

<u>The Wind Blew</u> - Pat Hutchins (Macmillan)

<u>Pelle's New Suit</u> - Elsa Beskow (Harper Collins)

Shared Reading:

"My New Baby" - Joan Phillips (<u>Beginning to Read, Book C</u>, Houghton Mifflin, <u>Literary Readers</u>)

Poems and Rhymes:

"The Tooth" - Lee Bennett Hopkins (Scholastic's <u>Literacy Place</u>)

"See Saw Margery Daw" - Mother Goose

Songs:

"Lloyd George Knew My Father" - <u>Wee Sing Silly Songs</u> (Price Stern Sloan)

Direct Instruction: ew

1. Write the word <u>new</u> on the board. Circle the "ew." Ask the children if they can tell you the sound these two letters represent. Tell them that the "w" acts as a vowel.

2. Write the following words on the board. Use blue for consonants and red for "ew."

   n<u>ew</u>   bl<u>ew</u>   ch<u>ew</u>   fl<u>ew</u>   gr<u>ew</u>   dr<u>ew</u>

3. Trace "ew" onto the carpet while making its sound.

Working With Letter and Sounds

1. Ask the children to draw three adjacent squares called *soundboxes* on their chalkboards or papers.

2. Dictate the following words: <u>blew</u>, <u>flew</u>, <u>grew</u>, <u>drew</u>, <u>crew</u>, <u>stew</u>.

   blew

b	l	ew

Unit VI
Lesson 9

Blend, Read and Write

1. Blend and read:

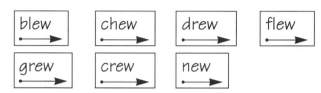

| blew → | chew → | drew → | flew → |
| grew → | crew → | new → | |

2. Write: Andrew has a new pen.

Word Construction

1. Ask the children to sort for the following letters (page 377):

| r | t | b | n | f | l | d | c | g | h | e | w |

2. Make these words: new, chew, blew, flew, drew, threw, crew, grew.

Books to Enhance Reading Comprehension, Skill and Language Development

Guided Reading:

"My New Boy" (Beginning to Read, Book C, Houghton Mifflin, Literary Readers) Practice reading this story with teacher guidance.

The Kite that Flew Away - Joanna Austin (Modern Curriculum Press, Ready Readers)

Independent Reading:

Add I Spy - Lucy Lawrence (Rigby)

Writing Frame:

We have a new _____

It is _____

It _____

I _____.

Make Your Own Little Books:

Beef Stew, pages 220-221. (Book 46)

Letter Cards for Word Construction (page 377)

Word Cards for Sentence Construction (page 378)

Tip:

Try to bring something new to school (book, toy, etc.). Let children write about it.

"This is not your stew,"
said Dan, Drew,
Jess and Dad.
"I know," said Mom.
"It is **your** stew.
I hope you like it."

8

Beef Stew*

* Idea adapted from "Mexicali Soup", a story
in Holt, Rinehart Basal Readers of the 1970s.

Name _____

1

✂ - ✂

"OK," said Mom. "I'll
see what I can do."

6

"Good," said Drew. "But
I don't like the potatoes."

3

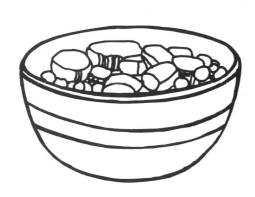

Mom said, "I will make
some beef stew."
"Good!" said Dan.
"But I don't like
the beef."

2

She left out the beef.
She left out the potatoes.
She left out the onions.
She left out the carrots.

7

"Good," said Jess. "But I
don't like the onions."

4

"Good," said Dad. "But I
don't like the carrots."

5

221
Reproducible

Unit VI
Lesson 10

Sight Vocabulary:

- Review <u>more</u>, <u>one</u>, <u>know</u>, <u>your</u>
- Introduce <u>would</u>
- Phonics and Structural Analysis: Review /ī/ i-e (kite); inflectional ending "-ed"; phonograms _ite _ide; wouldn't

Spelling: kite, bite, white, quite, ride, side, hide, wide

Grammar, Mechanics and Usage:

Speech marks, comma before "said," exclamation point and emphasis; past tense

Developing Phonemic Awareness,

Read Aloud:

<u>Chicken Soup With Rice</u> - Maurice Sendak (Harper)

<u>One Fine Day</u> - Nonny Hogrogrian (Macmillan)

<u>Mike Mulligan</u> - Virginia Lee Burton (Houghton Mifflin)

Shared Reading:

<u>Chicken Little</u> - Janet Hillman (Rigby, Big Book)

<u>Green Eggs and Ham</u> - Dr. Seuss (Harper)

Poems and Rhymes:

"The Kite" - <u>Beginning to Read, Book B</u> (Houghton Mifflin, <u>Literary Readers</u>)

"Banbury Cross" - Mother Goose

"Ride a Purple Pelican" - Jack Prelutsky in <u>Ride a Purple Pelican</u> (Greenwillow)

Song:

"And the Sidewalk Went All Around" (Wright Group, Big Book)

Direct Instruction: inflectional ending "ed."

1. Ask for someone to "help you." When the child comes to you, say, "Please look at something in the room and tell me what it is." When the child answers, write the sentence on the board:

    Veronica is looking at the book.

Unit VI
Lesson 10

Tip:

Show the children "ed" words that end in different sounds: <u>walked</u>, <u>started</u>, <u>burned</u>, etc. Let children classify them in the pocket chart.

Ask the child to take his or her seat. Then ask "What did Veronica look at?" Elicit the past tense.

    Veronica <u>looked</u> at the book.

Explain that we add "ed" to denote something that has taken place. Sometimes "ed" sounds like a "t."

2. Call on other children. Use verbs, such as <u>want</u>, <u>help</u>, <u>walk</u> and <u>talk</u>. Call attention to the fact "_ed" represents different sounds.

Working With Letters and Sounds

1. Ask the children to draw three adjacent squares called soundboxes on their chalkboards or papers.

2. Dictate the following words: <u>kite</u>, <u>bite</u>, <u>white</u>, <u>time</u>, <u>dime</u>, <u>lime</u>, <u>ride</u>, <u>side</u>, <u>wide</u>.

    kite

k	i	te

Blend, Read and Write

1. Blend and read:

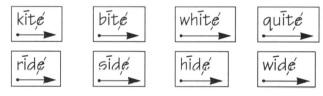

2. Write: Mike likes his kite.

Word Construction

1. Ask the children to sort for the following letters (page 379):

2. Make the following words: <u>kite</u>, <u>bite</u>, <u>white</u>, <u>quite</u>, <u>ride</u>, <u>side</u>, <u>hide</u>, <u>wide</u>.

Unit VI
Lesson 10

Books to Enhance Reading Comprehension, Skill and Language Development

Guided Reading:

"Boo Bear and the Kite" - David McPhail (<u>Beginning to Read, Book B</u> Houghton Mifflin, <u>Literary Readers</u>)

<u>Dive In!</u> - Lilly Ernesto (Modern Curriculum Press, <u>Ready Readers</u>)

Independent Reading:

Add "My New Boy" - (<u>Beginning to Read, Book C,</u> Houghton Mifflin, <u>Literary Readers</u>)

Activity for Home or School

Write the word <u>would</u> on an index card. Trace with crayon or glue. Take home to practice. Put one page from the book <u>Green Eggs and Ham</u> on the overhead projector for choral reading.

Writing Frame:

I would like to_____.

I would _____.

Make Your Own Little Books:

<u>I Would Like to Be</u>, pages 225-226. (Book 47)

Letter Cards for Word Construction (page 379)

Word Cards for Sentence Construction (page 380)

I would like to be a dad.
I would love my baby.

8

I Would Like to Be

Name _____

1

I would like to be
a firefighter.
I would help put
out the fires.

6

225
Reproducible

I would like to be
a trucker. I would
drive the big rigs.

3

I would like to be
a teacher.
I would teach the
kids to read.

2

I would like to be a cook
I would make good food

7

I would like to be a
policeman. I would
get the bad men.

4

I would like to be
a fisherman.
I would catch
a lot of fish.

5

Unit VI
Lesson 11

Sight Vocabulary:

- Review <u>more</u>, <u>one</u>, <u>know</u>, <u>your</u>
- Introduce <u>mother</u>
- Phonics and Structural Analysis: Review short u; inflectional ending "_ed"; aren't

Spelling: us, bus, just, must, fun, run, sun

Grammar, Mechanics and Usage: Present and past tenses.

Developing Phonemic Awareness

Read Aloud:

<u>A Chair for My Mother</u> - Vera Williams (Greenwillow)
<u>On Mother's Lap</u> - Ann Herbert Scott (Houghton Mifflin)

Shared Reading:

<u>Pumpkin Pumpkin</u> - Jeanne Titherington (<u>Beginning to Read, Book C</u>, Houghton Mifflin, <u>Literary Readers</u>)
<u>Good-Night, Owl!</u> - Pat Hutchins (Houghton Mifflin)
<u>The Little Red Hen</u> - Brenda Parkes (Rigby, Big Book)
<u>The Gingerbread Man</u> - Brenda Parkes (Rigby, Big Book)
<u>The Three Little Pigs</u> - Brenda Parkes (Rigby, Big Book)

Rhymes and Poems:

"The Little Turtle" - Vachel Lindsay (<u>Beginning to Read, Book B</u>, Houghton Mifflin, <u>Literary Readers</u>)
<u>Gobble, Gobble, Glup Glup</u> - Judith Smith (Rigby, Big Book)

Song:

"Found a Peanut" <u>Wee Sing Silly Songs</u> (Price Stern Sloan)

Direct Instruction: Present and Past Tense

1. Tell the children that you are going to write two sentences on the board that are <u>almost</u> the same. Ask them if they can find the difference. Write:

    > I talk to the teacher.
    > I talked to the teacher.

    Explain that "talk" refers to what is happening right now; whereas "talked" tells us that has happened already.

Unit VI
Lesson 11

2. Continue with other examples.

I <u>help</u> my mother.   A frog <u>wants</u> to come in.

I <u>helped</u> my mother.   A frog <u>wanted</u> to come in.

Working With Letters and Sounds

1. Ask the children to draw three adjacent squares called soundboxes on their chalkboards or papers.

2. Dictate the following words: <u>bus</u>, <u>sun</u>, <u>fun</u>, <u>run</u>, <u>bun</u>, <u>gun</u>, <u>gum</u>.

gum

Blend, Read and Write

1. Blend and read:

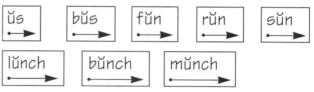

2. Write: Bud had lunch with us.

Word Construction

1. Ask the children to sort for the following letters (page 381):

2. Make these words: <u>us</u>, <u>bus</u>, <u>must</u>, <u>trust</u>, <u>crust</u>, <u>lunch</u>, <u>bunch</u>, <u>jump</u>.

Books to Enhance Reading Comprehension, Skill and Language Development

Guided Reading:

"Fox Gets Lunch" - James Marshall (<u>Beginning to Read</u>, Houghton Mifflin, <u>Literary Readers</u>)

<u>Little Red Hen</u> - Judy Nayer (Modern Curriculum Press, <u>Ready Readers</u>)

<u>Three Little Pigs</u> - Deana Kirk (Modern Curriculum Press, <u>Ready Readers</u>)

Independent Reading:

Add "Boo Bear and the Kite" - David McPhail (<u>Beginning to Read, Book B</u>, Houghton Mifflin, <u>Literary Readers</u>) and other beginning-to-read books.

Unit VI
Lesson 11

Tip:
Children get the words <u>was</u> and <u>saw</u> mixed up. You might want to put a dot under the first letter: ṣaw; ẉas. Also, stress context and meaning.

Activity for Home or School

Write the word <u>was</u> on an index card. Trace with crayon or glue. Take home to practice.

Writing Frame:

One day my mom_____.

We _____.

Make Your Own Little Books:

<u>The Tooth</u>, pages 230-231. (Book 48)

Letter Cards for Word Construction (page 381)

Word Cards for Sentence Construction (page 382)

Evaluation: Unit VI

Directions:

1. Ask each child to read the word lists and the sentences.

List A	List B
one	know
some	more
your	goes
was	or
other	would
mother	home
two	bee

Would you like to go home?

I know what you would like.

2. Dictate the following sentence: My mother will take me to the zoo.

The Tooth

dog bone!

8

Name _____

1

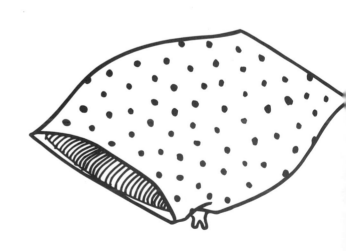

That night Sam
put the dog tooth
under his pillow.

6

"I will put the tooth
under my pillow.
The tooth fairy will
think it is **my** tooth."

3

Sam said, "Mother, my dog's tooth fell out. I know what I can do." "What?" asked Mother.

2

He went to sleep. When he woke up he looked under his pillow and saw a

7

"Why would you do that?" asked Mother.

4

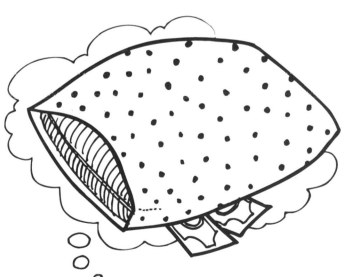

"The Tooth Fairy will bring me some money," said Sam. "Is that a good plan?" asked Mom.

5

Unit VII
Target Word
Recognition Skills:

u (found) /ī/ find, wild ar (far)

/s/ c (pencil) /ng/ long

_all, _ank, _ink, _ing

<u>there</u>, <u>friends</u>, <u>Mr.</u>, <u>any</u>,

<u>from</u>, <u>where</u>, <u>work</u>, <u>little</u>,

<u>Father</u>, <u>word</u>, <u>were</u>, <u>find</u>

Unit VII
Lesson 1

Sight Vocabulary: from

■ Phonics and Structural Analysis: /är/

Spelling: car, far, arm, farm, harm, dark, mark, park

Grammar, Mechanics and Usage:
The exclamation and exclamation point

Developing Phonemic Awareness

Read Aloud:
Is It Dark? Is It Light? - Mary C. Lankford (Scholastic)
Arthur books by Marc Brown (Little, Brown & Co.)

Shared Reading:
In a Dark Dark Wood (Wright Group, Big Book)

Rhymes:
"Hark, Hark, the Dogs Do Bark" - Mother Goose
"The Queen of Hearts" - Mother Goose

Songs:
"Smarty Pants" - Joy Cowley (Wright Group, Big Book and tape)
"Old MacDonald Had a Farm" - (North-South Books)
"BINGO" - Greg and Steve in We All Live Together, Volume IV
    (Youngheart Records)

Direct Instruction: /är/

1. Tell the children that when "R says its own name in a word, such as Arthur, it's spelled ar." Give the children examples of words that begin with r as opposed to words that begin with ar. Help them to note the difference.

r	ar
red	Arthur
rope	art
rug	arm
rat	article

2. Trace ar into the carpet while making the /är/ sound.

Working With Letters and Sounds

1. Ask the children to draw three adjacent squares called soundboxes on their chalkboards or papers.

farm

f	ar	m

2. Dictate these words: <u>farm</u>, <u>harm</u>, <u>mark</u>, <u>dark</u>, <u>bark</u>, <u>park</u>, <u>card</u>, <u>hard</u>.

Blend, Read and Write

1. Blend and read:

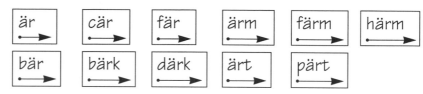

är →	cär →	fär →	ärm →	färm →	härm →

bär →	bärk →	därk →	ärt →	pärt →

2. Write: Mark has a dark car.

Word Construction

1. Ask the children to sort for the following letters (page 383):

c	<u>b</u>	k	<u>d</u>	h	<u>p</u>	m	f	a	r

2. Make these words: <u>car</u>, <u>card</u>, <u>hard</u>, <u>far</u>, <u>arm</u>, <u>farm</u>, <u>dark</u>, <u>park</u>.

Enhancing Reading Comprehension, Skill and Language Development

Guided Reading:

<u>Happy Birthday!</u> - Avelyn Davidson (Rigby)

<u>The Best Birthday Mole Ever Had</u> - Fay Robinson (Modern Curriculum Press, <u>Ready Readers</u>)

Independent Reading:

Add easy books that have been introduced to the class.

Writing Frame:

I had a party.

I _____.

My _____.

It was_____.

Make Your Own Little Books:

<u>The Surprise</u>, pages 235-236. (Book 49)

Letter Cards for Word Construction (page 383)

Word Cards for Sentence Construction (page 384)

There was a pony!
A pony for Mark and
Ann. "This pony is for
you," said Dad.
"Happy Birthday!"

8

The Surprise

Name _____

1

They went past the
dog and the cat.

6

235

When they got
to the farm, they
went past the pigs.

3

Mark and Ann
got in Dad's car.
Dad said, "We are
going to a farm."

2

They stopped at
the barn. "Let's take
a look," said Dad.

7

Then went past the cows.

4

236
Reproducible

They went past
the chickens.

5

Unit VII
Lesson 2

Sight Vocabulary:

- Review <u>from</u>
- Introduce <u>there</u>, <u>water</u>
- Phonics and Structural Analysis: /ou/ <u>found</u>;
  <u>ground</u>, <u>hound</u>, <u>mound</u>, <u>pound</u>, <u>round</u>, <u>sound</u>; <u>there's</u>

Spelling: out, our, round, sound, found, ground, pound

Grammar, Mechanics and Usage: Review conventions

Developing Phonemic Awareness

Read Aloud:
<u>Cloudy With a Chance of Meatballs</u> - Judi Barrett (Macmillan)
<u>Green Eggs and Ham</u> - Dr. Seuss (Random House)
<u>The Cat in the Hat</u> - Dr. Seuss (Random House)

Shared Reading:
<u>Mouse Paint</u> - Ellen Stoll Walsh (Big Book Edition)
<u>The Little Red Hen</u> - Brenda Parkes (Rigby, Big Book)

Rhymes and Poems:
<u>Time for Rhyme</u> (Rigby, Big Book)
<u>To Market To Market</u> (Wright Group, Big Book)

Song:
"Round in a Circle" - Greg and Steve in <u>We All Live Together, Volume 1</u>
   (Youngheart Records)

Direct Instruction: /ou/

1. Tell the children that you always think of the letters "ou" as the "hurt letters." Ask them to guess why. Explain that these two letters (when together) represent the sound people make when they are hurt - OW! Ouch!

2. Let children dramatize getting hurt and exclaiming "OW!" or "Ouch!"

3. Have students trace <u>ou</u> into the carpet as they make the /ou/ sound.

Working With Letters and Sounds

1. Ask the children to draw <u>four</u> adjacent squares called soundboxes on their chalkboards or papers.

2. Dictate the following words: <u>found</u>, <u>bound</u>, <u>mound</u>, <u>hound</u>, <u>pound</u>, <u>round</u>, <u>sound</u>. Guide children to write the letter or letters representing a single sound in one box.

found

f	ou	n	d

237

Unit VII
Lesson 2

Blend, Read and Write

1. Blend and read:

| out → | shout → | found → | ground → |

| sound → | pound → | our → |

2. Write: Pat found a hound dog.

Word Construction

1. Ask children to sort for the following letters (page 385):

| f | n | d | h | r | s | b | g | t | o | u | m | e |

2. Make these words: out, shout, found, hound, round, sound, bound, ground, mouse, house.

Books to Enhance Reading Comprehension, Skill and Language Development

Guided Reading:

Ouch! - Lucy Lawrence (Rigby)
In My Bed - Ron Bacon (Rigby)
Our Dog Sam - Ron Bacon (Rigby)
Squirrels - G. Clifford (Modern Curriculum Press, Ready Readers)

Independent Reading:

Add beginner books that have been introduced to the class.

Activity for Home or School: there

1. Write the word there on an index card. Trace over it with crayon or glue. Take home to practice.

2. Find a page from the book Green Eggs and Ham (Dr. Seuss, Random House) that has the word there on it. Copy the page onto a transparency for use on the overhead projector. Read it chorally with your class many times.

Writing Frame:

One day I found a _____.   Or   A _____ is round.
It _____.   A _____ is round.
I _____.   A _____ is round
_____.   but a _____ is not round.

Make Your Own Little Books:

Look What I Found! pages 239-240. (Book 50)

Letter Cards for Word Construction (page 385)

Word Cards for Sentence Construction (page 386)

238

Look What
I Found!

boat!

8

Name _____

1

ball!

6

239
Reproducible

It is a . . .

3

© Fearon Teacher Aids FE7948

Look! There's
something yellow.
I can write with it.

2

Look! There's something
blue. I can make it go
in the water. It is a . . .

7

pencil!

4

Look! There's something
blue. It is round. I can
bounce it. It is a . . .

5

240
Reproducible

Unit VII
Lesson 3

Sight Vocabulary:

- Review <u>from</u>, <u>there</u>
- Introduce <u>where</u>
- Phonics and Structural Analysis: /s/ "soft c" (ceiling); inflectional ending <u>ing</u>. "_ing"; "s"

Spelling: where, ice, mice, nice, face, lace, race

Grammar, Mechanics and Usage:

Observing punctuation in oral reading; action words (verbs)

Developing Phonemic Awareness

Read Aloud:

<u>Mice are Nice</u> - Judy Nayer (McClanahan)

<u>The Pop-Up Mice of Mr. Brice</u> - Theo Le Sieg (Random House)

<u>This Is the Place for Me</u> - Joanna Cole (Scholastic)

<u>Cinderella</u> - Charles Perrault, illustrated by Errol Le Cain (Puffin)

<u>The City Mouse and the Country Mouse</u> - Jan Brett

Shared Reading:

<u>The Snowy Day</u> - Ezra Jack Keats (Viking)

<u>Frederick</u> - Leo Lionni (Pantheon)

<u>Seven Blind Mice</u> - Ed Young (Scholastic <u>Literacy Place</u>, Big Book)

Rhymes and Poems:

<u>There Was a Place and Other Poems</u> - Myra Cohn Livingston (Macmillan)

"Mice"- Rose Fyleman in <u>Read Aloud Rhymes</u> (Alfred Knopf)

<u>Chicken Soup With Rice</u> - Maurice Sendak (Weston Woods)

"I Speak" - Arnold Shapiro in <u>Literary Reader, Book 1</u>, (Houghton Mifflin)

<u>Everytime I Climb a Tree</u> - David McCord (Little, Brown)

Song:

"Little Bunny Foo Foo" in <u>Wee Sing Silly Songs</u> (Price Stern Sloan)

Direct Instruction: Soft c

1. Explain to the children that sometimes the letter "c" stands for the "k" sound and sometimes it stands for the "s" sound. Tell them that there is a way to tell which is which and you want them to guess what it is. Ask the children "to make up a rule" as you write these words on the board. Read each word in the lists on page 242:

241

Unit VII
Lesson 3

Tip:

If children can be helped to see these patterns for themselves, they will probably remember them. Memorization of rules is inappropriate for young children.

Hard C		Soft C	
cute	cat	ceiling	race
cast	call	circus	face
can	picnic	place	ice
sick	cup	city	mice

The children should come to realize that soft "c" is always <u>followed</u> by "e" or "i."

2. Give children "hard c" and "soft c" words. Ask them to classify them with a partner.

Direct Instruction: inflectional ending "ing"

1. Ask for "helpers." When a child comes up, ask her to <u>do</u> something — <u>look</u>, <u>jump</u>, <u>walk</u> etc. When she does, write a sentence describing the action.

   Alex jumps.

   Then explain that you can write it another way:

   Alex is jumping.

   Draw the children's attention to the ending "ing." Ask them to spell the word <u>jumping</u> with you.

2. Call on other "helpers." Repeat the procedure several times.

3. Ask the children to look through books to find examples of "ing" words.

Working With Letters and Sounds

1. Ask the children to draw three adjacent squares called *soundboxes* on their chalkboards or papers.

2. Dictate the following words: <u>face</u>, <u>race</u>, <u>pace</u>, <u>lace</u>, <u>mice</u>, <u>nice</u>, <u>rice</u>, <u>dice</u>.

   face

f	a	c͇e͇

Ask children to draw a line through the final <u>e</u> to show that it is "silent." However, remind the children that the final "e" affects the sound of "a" or "i."

Blend, Read and Write

1. Blend and read:

| fāc͇e͇→ | rāc͇e͇→ | plāc͇e͇→ | mīc͇e͇→ | nīc͇e͇→ | slīc͇e͇→ |

2. Write: I think mice are nice.

Word Construction

1. Ask the children to sort for the following letters (page 397):

| f | c | e | r | <u>p</u> | l | m | <u>n</u> | i | s | a |

242

2. Make these words: <u>face</u>, <u>race</u>, <u>place</u>, <u>mice</u>, <u>nice</u>, <u>ice</u>, <u>space</u>, <u>lace</u>

Books to Enhance Reading Comprehension, Skill and Language Development

Guided Reading:

<u>All About Bats</u> - Jennifer Jacobson (Modern Curriculum Press, <u>Ready Readers</u>)

<u>The City Cat and the Country Cat</u> - Anne Miranda (Modern Curriculum Press, <u>Ready Readers</u>)

"The Pig and the Pencil" - James Marshall in <u>Beginning to Read, Book C</u> (Houghton Mifflin, <u>Literary Readers</u>)

Independent Reading:

Add beginner books that have been introduced to the children.

Activity for Home or School

Write the word <u>where</u> on an index card. Trace over it with glue or crayon. Take it home to practice.

Writing Frame:

Show children how to make flap books (as in <u>Where's Spot?</u> by Eric Hill).

Where's the [cat, dog, etc.]?

Is it [under the bed]?

Is it [behind the couch]?

Is it [on top of the table]?

Is it [in the closet]?

Example:

Is it under the bed?

Make Your Own Little Books:

<u>The City Mouse and the Country Mouse</u>, pages 244-245. (Book 51)

Letter Cards for Word Construction (page 387)

Word Cards for Sentence Construction (page 388)

after the City Mouse and the Country Mouse. "I am going home," said the City Mouse. And he did.

8

The City Mouse and the Country Mouse

adapted from Aesop

Name _____

1

 -

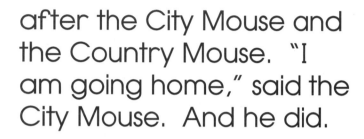

The food was good. "I like it at your house," said

6

The country mouse was glad to see him. "I do not have much to eat, but you may have some of it."

3

The city mouse went to
see the country mouse.

2

the country mouse.
"We can have a lot
to eat." Just then a
cat came in. He ran

7

The city mouse did not
like the food. "Come
to my house," he said.
"You will like it."

4

245
Reproducible

The country mouse and
the city mouse went to
the big city. They went
to a big house.

5 © Fearon Teacher Aids FE7948

Unit VII
Lesson 4

Sight Vocabulary:

- Review <u>from</u>, <u>there</u>, <u>where</u>
- Introduce <u>little</u>, <u>friends</u>, <u>work</u>, <u>Father</u>, <u>any</u>, <u>find</u>
- Phonics and Structural Analysis: /ô/ all _all, ball, call, fall, hall, mall, tall, wall; inflectional ending "_ed"

Spelling: little, work, all, ball, call, fall, tall, wall

Grammar, Mechanics and Usage:

Observing punctuation; words that name (nouns); proper nouns

Developing Phonemic Awareness

Read Aloud:

<u>Ira Sleeps Over</u> - Bernard Weber (Houghton Mifflin)

Shared Reading:

<u>Goldilocks and the Three Bears</u> - Brenda Parkes (Rigby, Big Book)

<u>The Lion and the Mouse</u> (Rigby, Big Book)

Rhymes and Poems:

"Ring Around the Rosie" - Mother Goose

"Thirty Days Hath September" - Mother Goose

Song:

"And the Sidewalk Went All Around" (Wright Group, Big Book)

Tip:

Children who do not "get" this need more practice hearing sounds within words. Do <u>lots</u> with rhymes, songs and word plays.

Direct Instruction: _all

1. Remind the children that if they learn one word, they can read many other words as well. Say, "If this is the word <u>all</u>, then this must be:"

<u>b</u>all   <u>m</u>all

<u>c</u>all   <u>t</u>all

<u>f</u>all   <u>w</u>all

<u>h</u>all

Unit VII Lesson 4

Word Construction:

1. Ask children to take the following letters out of their letter boxes (page 389):

| a | l | l | b | c | h | t | w | f |

2. Make these words: <u>ball</u>, <u>call</u>, <u>fall</u>, <u>hall</u>, <u>tall</u>, <u>wall</u>.

Books to Enhance Reading Comprehension, Skill and Language Development

Guided Reading:

"Boo Bear Takes a Rest" - David McPhail in <u>Beginning to Read, Book C</u> (Houghton Mifflin, <u>Literary Readers</u>.)

<u>A Lot Happened Today</u> - Judy Nayer (Modern Curriculum Press, <u>Ready Readers</u>)

<u>All Fall Down</u> - Brian Wildsmith (Oxford University Press)

<u>Carrots Can't Talk</u> - Kathryn E. Lewis (Modern Curriculum Press, <u>Ready Readers</u>)

Independent Reading:

Add beginner books that have been introduced to the class.

Writing Frame:

One time I _____.

First, I _____.

Then I _____.

Finally I _____.

Make Your Own Little Books:

<u>The Goose That Laid the Golden Egg</u>, pages 248-249. (Book 52)

Letter Cards for Word Construction (page 389)

Word Cards for Sentence Construction (page 390)

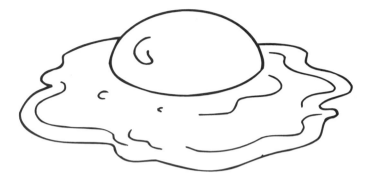

But inside the goose was not gold. The man and his wife never got another golden egg.

8

The Goose That Laid the Golden Eggs

adapted from Aesop

Name _____

1

✂ - ✂

"Yes, that's what we will do," said the wife.

6

So the man and his wife got very rich.

3

248
Reproducible

A man and his wife had a goose that laid golden eggs.

2

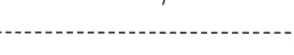

So they killed the goose.

7

The man and his wife had a lot of gold, but they wanted more.

4

"I know," said the man. "We can kill the goose and get all the gold inside."

5   © Fearon Teacher Aids FE7948

Unit VII Lesson 5

<u>Sight Vocabulary:</u>

- Review <u>Father</u>, <u>little</u>, <u>friends</u>, <u>work</u>, <u>from</u>, <u>there</u>, <u>where</u>
- Introduce <u>Mr.</u>, <u>were</u>
- Phonics and Structural Analysis: /ng/; phonogram _ing (king, ring, sing, wing, thing, bring); doubling the final consonant before adding "ed."

Spelling: sing, ring, thing, bring, king, wing

Grammar, Mechanics and Usage: Abbreviations; the command

Developing Phonemic Awareness

Read Aloud:

<u>If I Were You</u> - Brian Wildsmith (Oxford University Press)

<u>Too Many Tamales</u> - Gary Soto (Harcourt Brace)

Shared Reading:

<u>Caps for Sale</u> - Esphyr Slobodkina (Addison-Wesley, Big Book)

<u>The Doorbell Rang</u> - Pat Hutchins (Scholastic, <u>Literacy Place</u>)

Rhymes and Poems:

"Sing a Song of Sixpence" - Mother Goose

"Introduction to Song of Innocence" - William Blake (in <u>The Random House Book of Poetry for Children</u>)

Song:

<u>Sing a Song</u> - June Melser (Wright Group, Big Book and cassette)

<u>Direct Instruction: /ng/ ing</u>

1. Tell the children that the <u>ng</u> at the end of <u>ing</u> blend together to make one sound — "it's the sound you hear at the end of <u>ding dong</u>."

2. Let the children pretend to ring bells while saying, "Ding, dong."

Blend, Read and Write

1. Blend and read:

2. Write: Bring the ring to me.

Unit VII
Lesson 5

Word Construction

1. Ask the children to sort for the following letters (page 391):

s	i	n	g	w	r	b	k	t	h

2. Make these words: <u>sing</u>, <u>ring</u>, <u>thing</u>, <u>wing</u>, <u>sting</u>, <u>bring</u>, <u>king</u>, <u>string</u>.

Books to Enhance Reading Comprehension, Skill and Language Development

Guided Reading:

<u>A Pig Can't Do a Thing</u> - Carolyn Clark (Modern Curriculum Press, <u>Ready Readers</u>)

<u>The Fox and the Crow</u> - Deb Eaton (Modern Curriculum Press, <u>Ready Readers</u>)

"Mr. Robot" - Laurene Krasny Brown in <u>Beginning to Read, Book C</u> (Houghton Mifflin, <u>Literary Readers</u>)

Independent Reading:

Add beginner books that have been presented to the class.

Writing Frame:

"Spring"

Spring is _____.

It is _____.

It _____.

I _____.

Make Your Own Little Books:

<u>Spring</u>, pages 252-253. (Book 53)

Letter Cards for Word Construction (page 391)

Word Cards for Sentence Construction (page 392)

Evaluation: Unit VII

Directions:

Ask each child to read the words and the sentences.

List A	List B
there	friends
Mr.	any
from	where
work	little
Father	all
were	word

All the boys and girls were walking to the park.

I put all my things away.

in the spring!

8

Spring

Name _____

1

 -

I can play ball.

6

I can see so many things.

3

Reproducible

I love spring!

2

I can feel like a king . . .

7

I can play with
my friends.

4

I can hear the birds sing.

5

253
Reproducible

Unit VIII

Target Word
Recognition Skills:

_ake _old squ_ _y (funny)
ir _igh ōo (moon) (June)
aw, au (all, saw) air _ly (happily)
le (bubble) wr oi, oy
<u>once</u>, <u>upon</u>, <u>bread</u>, <u>who</u>, <u>could</u>,
<u>would</u>, <u>again</u>, <u>talk</u>, <u>walk</u>, <u>very</u>,
<u>happy</u>, <u>through</u>, <u>noise</u>, <u>thought</u>,
<u>were</u>, <u>buy</u>, <u>many</u>, <u>pull</u>, <u>because</u>

Unit VIII
Lesson 1

Sight Vocabulary:

- Introduce <u>once</u>, <u>upon</u>, <u>bread</u>, <u>who</u>
- Phonics and Structural Analysis:
  initial consonant substitution; phonogram
  _ake; compound words (upon, into)

Spelling: bake, cake, fake, lake, make, shake, quake, rake, take, wake

Grammar, Mechanics and Usage:
Speech marks, comma before "said"

Developing Phonemic Awareness

Read Aloud:
<u>Make Way for the Ducklings</u> - Robert McCloskey (Viking)
<u>The Cake That Mack Ate</u> - Rose Robart (Little, Brown)
<u>What Rhymes With Snake?</u> - Rick Brown (Tambourine Books)

Shared Reading:
<u>The Little Red Hen</u> - Brenda Parkes (Rigby, Big Book)
<u>Rosie's Walk</u> - Pat Hutchins (Macmillan, Big Book)

Rhymes and Poems:
<u>Time for a Rhyme</u> - (Rigby, Big Book)
"Pat-a-Cake" - Mother Goose

Song:
<u>Lazy Mary</u> - June Melser (Wright Group, Big Book and Tape)

Direct Instruction: ake

1. Remind the children that there are many words that are exactly alike except for the beginning. Tell them if they learn <u>one</u> of these words, they will automatically know many others. Tell them that the word <u>make</u> is one of those words.

2. Write the word <u>make</u> on the board. Erase the "m" and say, "I erased the 'm.' Now write 'b.' The word is _____. Yes, bake." Continue this with <u>cake</u>, <u>rake</u>, <u>sake</u>, <u>lake</u>, <u>brake</u>, <u>flake</u>, etc.

Working With Letters and Sounds
1. Ask the children to draw three adjacent squares called *soundboxes* on their chalkboards or papers.

2. Dictate these words: <u>cake</u>, <u>make</u>, <u>rake</u>, <u>bake</u>, <u>take</u>, <u>wake</u>, <u>shake</u>.

   shake

sh	a	ke̸

255

Unit VIII
Lesson 1

Blend, Read and Write

1. Blend and read:

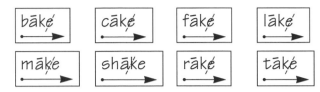

| bāke → | cāke → | fāke → | lāke → |
| make → | shake → | rāke → | tāke → |

2. Write: We will bake a cake.

Word Construction

1. Ask the children to sort for the following letters (page 393):

| c | a | k | e | b̲ | l | t | r | q̲ | u̲ | f | s | h |

2. Make these words: <u>cake</u>, <u>back</u>, <u>fake</u>, <u>lake</u>, <u>take</u>, <u>rake</u>, <u>shake</u>, <u>quake</u>.

Books to Enhance Reading Comprehension, Skill and Language Development

Guided Reading:

<u>What's Inside?</u> - Mary Jane Martin (Scholastic, <u>Literacy Place</u>)

<u>The Farm</u> - Claudia Logan (Modern Curriculum Press, <u>Ready Readers</u>)

"The Little Red Hen" - Jan Brett (in Houghton Mifflin, <u>Literary Readers, Book 1</u>)

<u>Pancakes</u> - Judy Nayer (Modern Curriculum Press, <u>Ready Readers</u>)

Independent Reading:

Add other beginner books that have been introduced to the class.

Writing Frame:

Stress beginning, middle, end. Let children retell a tale, if they prefer.

Once upon a time _____

_____.

Make Your Own Little Books:

<u>The Little Red Hen</u>, pages 257-258. (Book 54)

Letter Cards for Word Construction (page 393)

Word Cards for Sentence Construction (page 394)

"Then I will do it myself,"
said the little red hen.
"And I will eat it myself,
too." And she did.

8

The Little Red Hen

Traditional

Name _____

1

"Then I will do it myself,"
said the little red hen.
And she did.

6

"Who will help me plant
the wheat?" she asked.
"Not I," said the dog.
"Not I," said the cat.
"Not I," said the duck.

3

Once upon a time there was a little red hen. One day she found some wheat.

2

"Who will help me make the bread?" asked the little red hen.
"Not I," said the dog.
"Not I," said the cat.
"Not I," said the duck.

7

"Then I will do it myself" said the little red hen. And she did.

4

"Who will help me cut the wheat?" asked the little red hen.
"Not I," said the dog.
"Not I," said the cat.
"Not I," said the duck.

5

Unit VIII
Lesson 2

Sight Vocabulary:

- Review <u>once</u>, <u>upon</u>, <u>bread</u>, <u>who</u>
- Introduce <u>could</u>, <u>would</u>, <u>again</u>
- Phonics and Structural Analysis: phonogram _old; compound words

Spelling: old, fold, gold, hold, sold, told

Grammar, Mechanics and Usage:
Review conventions. Teach past tense.

Developing Phonemic Awareness

Read Aloud:

<u>The Gingerbread Man</u> - Paul Galdone (Scholastic)

<u>Stone Soup</u> - Marcia Brown (Scribner)

<u>Green Eggs and Ham</u> - Dr. Seuss (Random House)

Shared Reading:

<u>Rumpelstiltskin</u> - Brenda Parkes (Rigby, Big Book)

Rhymes:

"Old King Cole" - Mother Goose
"Old Mother Hubbard" - Mother Goose

Song:

"This Old Man" - Raffi in <u>Baby Beluga</u> (MCA)

Direct Instruction: phonogram _old

1. Remind children that if they know <u>one</u> word, they can figure out many others by changing the first letter or letters. Tell them that <u>old</u> is such a word.

2. Say, "If I put a <u>g</u> in front of <u>old</u>, I have _____. Yes, <u>gold</u>. If I take away the <u>g</u> and put an <u>f</u>, I have _____. Right, <u>fold</u>." Do this with <u>mold</u>, <u>bold</u>, <u>told</u>, <u>hold</u>, <u>scold</u>, <u>sold</u>, etc.

Working With Letters and Sounds

1. Ask the children to make <u>four</u> adjacent squares called soundboxes on their chalkboards or papers.

2. Dictate the following words: <u>gold</u>, <u>fold</u>, <u>bold</u>, <u>cold</u>, <u>told</u>, <u>sold</u>, <u>hold</u>, <u>told</u>.

told

t	o	l	d

Unit VIII
Lesson 2

Blend, Read and Write

1. Blend and read:

| ōld → | bōld → | cōld → | fōld → |
| gōld → | hōld → | sōld → | tōld → |

2. Write: The old man sold his car.

Word Construction

1. Ask the children to sort for the following letters (page 395):

| b | o | s | d | f | g | h | m | l | t | c |

2. Make these words: bold, cold, fold, gold, hold, mold, sold, told.

Books to Enhance Reading Comprehension, Skill and Language Development

Guided Reading:

"The Enormous Turnip" - Alexei Tolstoy (Houghton Mifflin, Literary Readers, Book 1)

Three Wishes - Polly Peterson (Modern Curriculum Press, Ready Readers)

Independent Reading:

Add beginner books that have been introduced to the class.

Writing Frame:

(based on the story "The Gingerbread Man")

Once upon a time _____

_____.

The gingerbread man _____

_____.

He _____.

Finally _____.

Make Your Own Little Books:

The Fox and the Grapes, pages 261-262. (Book 55)

Letter Cards for Word Construction (page 395)

Word Cards for Sentence Construction (page 396)

"Oh, well," he said. "The grapes will be sour. I don't want them anyway."

8

The Fox and the Grapes

adapted from Aesop

Name _____

1

The fox jumped up as far as he could . . .

6

those grapes," he said. The fox jumped but he could not get the grapes.

3 © Fearon Teacher Aids FE7948

One day a fox saw
some big fat grapes
on a grapevine.
"I will try to get

2

but he could not
get the grapes.

7

He jumped again.
He still could not
get the grapes.

4

262

"I will jump one more
time," said the fox.

5

Unit VIII
Lesson 3

Sight Vocabulary:

- Review <u>once</u>, <u>upon</u>, <u>bread</u>, <u>who</u>
- Introduce <u>talk</u>, <u>walk</u>
- Phonics and Structural Analysis: squ_; "ing" ending

Spelling: walk, talk

Grammar, Mechanics and Usage:

Speech balloons; present tense

Developing Phonemic Awareness

Read Aloud:

<u>I Went Walking</u> - Sue Williams (Harcourt)

<u>Little Red Riding Hood</u> - Trina Schart Hyman (Holiday House)

<u>Taily-Po</u> - Joanna Galdone (Houghton Mifflin)

Shared Reading:

<u>Jack and the Beanstalk</u> - Judith Smith (Rigby, Big Book)

<u>Good-Night, Owl!</u> - Pat Hutchins (Macmillan, Big Book)

Rhymes and Poems:

<u>To Market, To Market</u> (Wright Group, Big Book)

"Sign a Song of People" - Lois Lenski (in the <u>Random House Book of Poetry for Children</u>)

Songs:

"Walk, Walk" - Raffi in <u>Rise and Shine</u> (Troubadour Records, Ltd.)

"The Boogie Walk" - Greg and Steve in <u>We All Live Together, Volume 2</u> (Youngheart Records)

Direct Instruction: squ

1. Tell the children a spooky story that has the word "squeak" in it. A good one is <u>Taily-Po</u>, retold by Joanna Galdone (Houghton Mifflin, 1977). Emphasize <u>squeak</u> to make it sound spooky: **Squeak**.

2. Ask, "How do you think 'squeak' is spelled?" Elicit different responses. Explain that "skw" or "scw" represent these sounds, but the usual spelling is <u>squ</u>.

3. Ask the children to help you make a chart of <u>squ</u> words. Let the children practice the words during independent reading or center time.

263

Unit VIII
Lesson 3

Blend, Read and Write

1. Blend and read:

| squeak | squeal | squeeze |
| squint | squish | squirt |

2. Write: A mouse can squeak.

Books to Enhance Reading Comprehension, Skill and Language Development

Guided Reading:

A Pot of Stone Soup - Robert R. O'Brien (Modern Curriculum Press, Ready Readers)

Bedtime at Aunt Carmen's - Carrie Nicholson (Modern Curriculum Press, Ready Readers)

Rosie's Walk - Pat Hutchins (Macmillan)

Independent Reading:

Add beginning-to-read books that have been introduced to the class.

Writing Frame:

(Based on the story "Little Red Riding Hood.")

Little Red Riding Hood _____

_____.

She _____.

The wolf _____.

At the end_____

_____.

Make Your Own Little Books:

The Mice and the Cat, pages 265-266. (Book 56)

Letter Cards for Word Construction (page 397)

Word Cards for Sentence Construction (page 398)

And no one did.

8

The Mice and the Cat

adapted from Aesop

Name _____

1

- -

the cat's neck?"
"I won't," said the
first mouse.

6

away from us," said one
mouse. "We can put a
bell around his neck.
Then we will know when
the cat is near."

3

One day the mice had a talk about the cat. "I know how we can keep the cat

2

"I won't," said the second mouse. "I won't," said the third mouse. "I won't," said the fourth mouse. "I won't," said the wise, old mouse.

7

"What a good plan," said the other mice. "Let's do it!"

4

Then one wise, old mouse said, "That is a good plan, but who will put the bell around

5

Sight Vocabulary:

- Review <u>once</u>, <u>upon</u>, <u>bread</u>, <u>who</u>, <u>talk</u>, <u>walk</u>
- Introduce <u>very</u>, <u>happy</u>
- Phonics and Structural Analysis: _y (happy); inflectional ending <u>ing</u>; contraction <u>it's</u>; doubling the final consonant before adding "y"; hearing syllables in words

Spelling: fun, funny, sun, sunny, pup, puppy, run, runny

Grammar, Mechanics and Usage:

Words that describe (adjectives)

Developing Phonemic Awareness

Read Aloud:

<u>Harry the Dirty Dog</u> - Gene Zion (Harper)
<u>The Very Busy Spider</u> - Eric Carle (Philomel)

Shared Reading:

<u>The Three Billy Goats Gruff</u> - Judith Smith (Rigby, Big Book)
<u>Lazy Mary</u> - Joy Cowley (Wright Group, Big Book)

Rhymes:

"Humpty Dumpty" - Mother Goose
"Lucy Locket" - Mother Goose

Songs:

"Teddy Bear Hug" - Raffi in <u>Everything Grows</u> (MCA)
"Hokey Pokey" - Greg and Steve in <u>Kidding Around With Greg and Steve</u> (Youngheart Records)

Direct Instruction: y (e)

1. Tell the children that you will write some of their names on the board. Ask them to raise their hands if they can read the names. Then write the children's names that end with "y" (if there are none, choose very familiar names or words as examples). Say to the children, "All these names end with <u>y</u>, but the <u>y</u> sounds like an <u>e</u>. What would your name sound like if <u>it</u> ended with an <u>e</u>?"

2. Play with names to make "nicknames" — Keithy, Sethy, Gracey, Jenny, etc.

Unit VIII
Lesson 4

Working With Letters and Sounds

1. Tell the children that you are going to write some words on the board. Explain that you will add "y" to each word, but you will do something else, too. Encourage them to guess what it is. Write these words in two columns. Use each word in a sentence:

sun	sunny
run	runny
fun	funny

2. When someone guesses that you doubled the "n," continue with other words that follow the same pattern (pup, flop, Dan, Ted, etc.). Challenge the children to discover the rule for themselves.

3. Ask the children to listen for syllables in words. Have them clap once for one syllable, twice for two, three times for three syllables and so forth. Explain that a <u>syllable</u> is a word or a part of a word that has a vowel sound in it.

Blend, Read and Write

1. Blend and read:

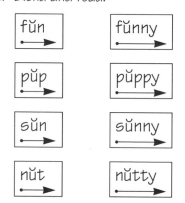

2. Write: I saw a funny puppy.

Word Construction

1. Ask the children to sort for the following letters (page 399):

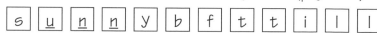

2. Make the following words: <u>sunny</u>, <u>funny</u>, <u>bunny</u>, <u>silly</u>, <u>nutty</u>, <u>sun</u>, <u>fun</u>, <u>nut</u>.

Unit VIII
Lesson 4

Books to Enhance Reading Comprehension, Skill and Language Development

Guided Reading:

<u>Funny Faces and Funny Places</u> - Mindy Menschell (Modern Curriculum Press, <u>Ready Readers</u>)

"Sleepy Bear" - Lydia Dabcavich in <u>Beginning to Read, Book A</u> (Houghton Mifflin, <u>Literacy Readers</u>)

Independent Reading:

Add beginning-to-read books that have been introduced to the class.

Writing Frame:

(Based on the story "The Three Billy Goats Gruff.")

Have the children fold their papers into six parts. Let them draw what happens <u>first</u> (first box), <u>last</u> (last box) and middle (middle parts). Have them write a sentence below each picture.

Once upon a time_____.

The first billy-goat _____.

The second billy-goat_____.

The third billy goat_____.

Finally_____

_____.

Make Your Own Little Books:

<u>The New Puppy</u>, pages 270-271. (Book 57)

Letter Cards for Word Construction (page 399)

Word Cards for Sentence Construction (page 400)

"Mom, now the puppy will be good."

8

The New Puppy

Name _____

1

He was wetting all over the house.

6

The puppy had a spot on his nose. He was very funny.

3

Ann had a new puppy.
She was very happy.

2

Mom was not happy
with the puppy.
Ann had a plan.

7

He was running
and jumping.

4

He was digging
in the yard.

5 © Fearon Teacher Aids FE7948

Unit VIII
Lesson 5

Sight Vocabulary:

- Review <u>once</u>, <u>upon</u>, <u>bread</u>, <u>who</u>, <u>talk</u>, <u>walk</u>
- Introduce <u>through</u>, <u>noise</u>, <u>donkey</u>, <u>monkey</u>
- Phonics and Structural Analysis: /oi/ oi, oy

Spelling: boy, toy, joy, Roy

Grammar, Mechanics and Usage:
Review conventions, nouns and proper names (capitalization of proper nouns)

Developing Phonemic Awareness

Read Aloud:
Read several versions of <u>Too Much Noise</u> so students can compare and contrast.
"Too Much Noise" - Ann McGovern (Houghton Mifflin, <u>Literary Readers, Book 1</u>)
"Song of the Witches" - William Shakespeare (<u>The Random House Book of Poetry for Children</u>)

Shared Reading:
"My New Boy" - Joan Phillips (<u>Beginning to Read, Book C</u>, Houghton Mifflin, <u>Literary Readers</u>)

Poem:
"Pierre" - Maurice Sendak (Scholastic, <u>Literacy Place</u>)

Song:
"Let's Make Some Noise" - Raffi in <u>Everything Grows</u> (MCA)

Direct Instruction: /oi/ oi, oy

1. Explain to the children that sometimes two letters combine to make one completely new sound. Tell them that <u>oi</u> and <u>oy</u> are two such examples. Say "<u>oy</u> stands for this sound /oi/ as in <u>boy</u>; <u>oi</u> stands for the same sound as in <u>boil</u>." (I have found that the children are quite amused by this sound, so I say it over and over again: <u>oi</u> <u>oi</u> <u>oi</u>).

2. Let the children go on a classroom "hunt" for <u>oi</u>, <u>oy</u> words. Each time they find a word, they are to write it on their clipboards or in notebooks. Use the children's list to make a class chart of <u>oi</u>, <u>oy</u> words.

3. Let the children pretend to be "little pigs." They'll enjoy crawling around the floor while squealing, "oink, oink, oink."

4. Have the children trace <u>oi</u> and <u>oy</u> into the carpet while making the sound these letters represent.

272

Unit VIII
Lesson 5

Working With Letters and Sounds

1. Prepare the following letter cards (page 401) for the pocket chart. Write the consonants in black and the vowels in red.

j	b	t	R	l	c	o	i	y

2. Say the word boy. Ask, "What letter comes first? What comes next?" Place the letters on the chart. Help the children see that only two sounds are represented by three letters.

b	oy

3. Continue with the following words: toy, Roy, joy, oil, boil, coil. Do this activity with the children.

Word Construction

1. Ask the children to sort for the following letters (page 401):

o	i	l	s	p	b	t	c	f	n	r

2. Make the following words: oil, spoil, toil, coil, boil, coin, broil, foil.

Books to Enhance Reading Comprehension, Skill and Language Development

Guided Reading:

"Too Much Noise" - Ann McGovern (Houghton Mifflin, Literary Readers, Book 1)

Independent Reading:

Add easy books that have been introduced to the class.

Writing Frame:

(Based on the story "Too Much Noise.")

The old man _____.

The wise man _____.

The old man got _____.

He _____.

Finally _____.

Make Your Own Little Books:

Too Much Noise, pages 274-275. (Book 58)

Letter Cards for Word Construction (page 401)

Word Cards for Sentence Construction (page 402)

273

Too Much Noise

"Ah. This is much better!"

8

Name _____

1

"Boys, you are making too much noise. Please make something else."

6

"Boys, you are making too much noise. Please listen to some other music."

3

"Boys, you are making too much noise. Play with some other toys."

2

"I know what I can do!"

7

"Boys, you are making too much noise. Please put the baby down."

4

"Boys, you are making too much noise. Please watch something else on TV."

5

Unit VIII
Lesson 6

Sight Vocabulary:

- Review <u>through</u>, <u>talk</u>, <u>walk</u>, <u>who</u>, <u>once</u>, <u>upon</u>
- Introduce <u>every</u>, <u>thought</u>
- Phonics and Structural Analysis: /ī/ igh; phonogram _ight; hearing syllables in words

Spelling: fight, light, might, night, right, sight, tight

Grammar, Mechanics and Usage:

Review conventions; plurals

Developing Phonemic Awareness

Shared Reading:

<u>The Hobyahs</u> - Brenda Parkes (Rigby, Big Book)

<u>There's a Nightmare in My Closet</u> - Mercer Mayer (Dial)

Poem:

"Good Night, Good Night" - Dennis Lee (<u>Beginning to Read, Book A</u>, Houghton Mifflin, <u>Literary Readers</u>)

Song:

"One Light, One Sun" - Raffi in <u>Evergreen Everblue</u> (Troubadour Records Ltd.)

Direct Instruction: /ī/ igh

1. Say to the children, "Many people think English is a difficult language to learn. See if you can guess why." Write the word "night" on the board. Read it for the class. Keep giving clues until someone suggests that you can't hear the "gh" in <u>night</u>, which might make it confusing to people who are learning the language.

2. Using a black pen for the initial and final consonants and red for "igh," write the following words on the board:

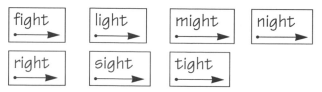

3. Help the children to use initial consonant substitution to decode these words.

Unit VIII
Lesson 6

Working With Letters and Sounds

1. Prepare these letter cards for the pocket chart. Write the <u>consonants</u> in black and <u>igh</u> in red .

| r | t | m | s | f | l | i | g | h |

2. Ask the children to help you spell the following words on the pocket chart: <u>right</u>, <u>might</u>, <u>fight</u>, <u>light</u>, <u>tight</u>, <u>sight</u>. Help them to see that there are three sounds represented by five letters. (The important concept here is the fact that the number of letters is not necessarily equal to the number of sounds in a word.)

Word Construction

1. Ask the children to sort for the following letters (page 403):

| <u>b</u> | r | i | g | h | t | s | r | l | m | <u>n</u> | t |

2. Make the following words: <u>bright</u>, <u>right</u>, <u>sight</u>, <u>right</u>, <u>light</u>, <u>might</u>, <u>night</u>, <u>tight</u>.

Books to Enhance Reading Comprehension, Skill and Language Development

Guided Reading:

<u>At Night</u> - Marcia Vaughan (Rigby)

<u>The Night Sky</u> - Patricia Ann Lynch (Modern Curriculum Press, <u>Ready Readers</u>)

Independent Reading:

Add easy books that have been introduced to the class.

Writing Frame:

"A Nightmare"

One night I had a nightmare. I

_____

_____.

Make Your Own Little Books:

<u>A Scary Night</u>, pages 278-279. (Book 59)

Letter Cards for Word Construction (page 403)

Word Cards for Sentence Construction (page 404)

Mom was there!

8

A Scary Night

Name _____

1

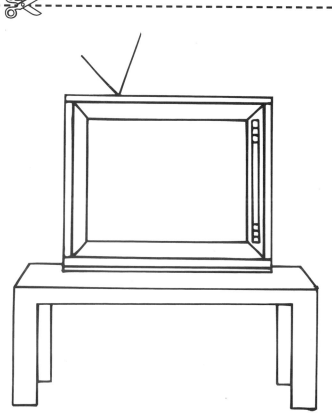

I looked in the TV room.
No one was there.

6

in the bedroom.
No one was there.

3

One night I thought I
heard a ghost. I looked

2

I looked in the kitchen . . .

7

I looked in the
living room. No
one was there.

4

I looked in the bathroom.
No one was there.

5

279

Unit VIII
Lesson 7

Sight Vocabulary:

- Review <u>once</u>, <u>upon</u>, <u>bread</u>, <u>who</u>, <u>walk</u>, <u>talk</u>, <u>every</u>, <u>thought</u>
- Introduce <u>were</u>, <u>buy</u>; <u>pull</u> (pulled)
- Phonics and Structural Analysis: /er/ ir, er, ur, ear (earth)

Spelling: girl, first, bird, third

Grammar, Mechanics and Usage: Comma in a series

Developing Phonemic Awareness

Read Aloud:
<u>Caps for Sale</u> - Esphyr Slobodkina (Harper Collins)
<u>Peter Rabbit</u> - Beatrix Potter (Puffin)
<u>Frederick</u> - Leo Lionni (Pantheon)

Shared Reading:
<u>The Fisherman and His Wife</u> - Pauline Cartwright (Rigby, Big Book)
<u>The Enormous Watermelon</u> - Brenda Parkes (Rigby, Big Book)

Rhymes and Poems:
<u>The Farm Concert</u> - Joy Cowley (Wright Group, Big Book)
<u>Time For a Rhyme</u> - (Rigby, Big Book)
<u>Time For a Number Rhyme</u> - (Rigby, Big Book)

Song:
"Little Sir Echo" - Greg and Steve in <u>We All Live Together, Volume I</u> (Youngheart Records)

Direct Instruction: /er/

1. Tell the children that you once knew a girl named Irma. You always remember the name because the little girl's mother would always call her in for dinner by shouting her name so all could hear.

     "<u>Ir</u> ma!" "<u>Ir</u> ma!"

2. Write "Irma" on the board. Explain that the first sound can be represented by several different spellings: <u>er</u>, <u>ir</u>, <u>ear</u> and <u>ur</u>. Ask the children to find as many words as they can with these letter combinations. Have them copy the words onto index cards.

Unit VIII
Lesson 7

3. Let the children help you classify these words on the pocket chart.

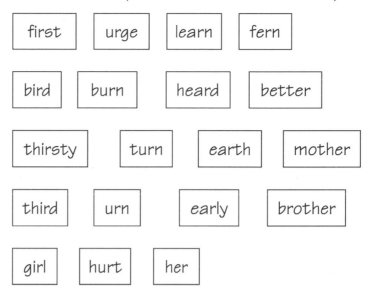

| first | urge | learn | fern |

| bird | burn | heard | better |

| thirsty | turn | earth | mother |

| third | urn | early | brother |

| girl | hurt | her |

Tip:
This might be too much for your students. If so, start with <u>ir</u> and take other letters at another time.

Blend, Read and Write

1. Blend and read:

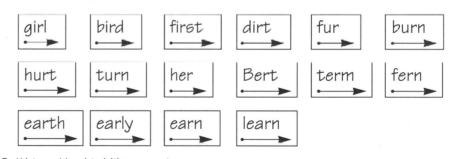

| girl → | bird → | first → | dirt → | fur → | burn → |

| hurt → | turn → | her → | Bert → | term → | fern → |

| earth → | early → | earn → | learn → |

2. Write: Her bird likes to sing.

Word Construction

1. Ask the children to sort for the following letters (page 405):

| f | i | r | s | t | <u>d</u> | <u>b</u> | h |

2. Make the following words: <u>fir</u>, <u>sir</u>, <u>first</u>, <u>third</u>, <u>shirt</u>, <u>dirt</u>, <u>bird</u>, <u>birth</u>.

Unit VIII
Lesson 7

Books to Enhance Reading Comprehension, Skill and Language Development

Guided Reading:

The Enormous Turnip - Alexei Tolstoy (Houghton Mifflin, Literary Readers, Book 1)

"The Man and His Caps" in "Selection Response Booklet" (Houghton Mifflin, Literary Readers, Book 1)

My Fish Does Not Chirp - Anne Tyler (Modern Curriculum Press, Ready Readers)

Sione's Talo - Lino Nelisi (Scholastic, Literacy Place)

Independent Reading:

Add beginning-to-read books that have been introduced to the class.

Writing Frame:

(Based on the story "Caps for Sale")

One day _____

First_____

Then _____

Next_____

Finally the man _____.

Make Your Own Little Books:

The Enormous Pumpkin, pages 283-284. (Book 60)

Letter Cards for Word Construction (page 405)

Word Cards for Sentence Construction (page 406)

© Fearon Teacher Aids FE7948

pulled the old woman.
The old woman pulled
the old man.
The old man pulled
the pumpkin.
And UP it came!

8

The Enormous Pumpkin

based on an old Russian tale

Name _____

1

So the old woman
called the little boy.
The little boy pulled
the old woman.
The old woman
pulled the old man.
The old man pulled the
pumpkin. They pulled

6

So the pumpkin seed
grew and grew
and grew until it was
<u>enormous</u>. The old
man tried to pull it up.

3

One day an old man
planted a pumpkin seed
and said, "Grow, grow,
little pumpkin seed."

2

and pulled and
pulled, but they
could not pull it up.
So the little boy
called the little girl.
The little girl pulled the
little boy. The little boy

7

He pulled and pulled
and pulled, but he
could not pull it up.
So the old man called
the old woman to help.

4

The old woman pulled
the old man.
The old man pulled
the pumpkin.
They pulled and
pulled and pulled,
but the pumpkin
would not come up.

5

Unit VIII
Lesson 8

Sight Vocabulary:

- Review <u>once</u>, <u>upon</u>, <u>bread</u>, <u>who</u>, <u>talk</u>, <u>walk</u>, <u>every</u>, <u>were</u>, <u>buy</u>, <u>thought</u>
- Introduce <u>many</u>
- Phonics and Structural Analysis: /oo/ ew, ue, ui, u-e, oo

Spelling: use, true, blue, chew, threw, moon, soon

Grammar, Mechanics and Usage:

Bold print for emphasis, exclamations and exclamation point; plural <u>es</u> (wish<u>es</u>)

Developing Phonemic Awareness

Read Aloud:

<u>The Wind Blew</u> - Pat Hutchins (Scholastic)

<u>Stellaluna</u> - Janell Cannon (Scholastic)

Shared Reading:

<u>Puss in Boots</u> - Janet Hillman (Rigby, Big Book)

<u>Teeny Tiny</u> - (Houghton Mifflin, Big Book)

Rhymes and Poems:

"Who Has Seen the Wind" - Christina Rossetti, <u>Poems to Read to the Very Young</u> (Random House)

<u>The Farm Concert</u> - Joy Cowley (Wright Group, Big Book)

Songs:

"Over in the Meadow" - Alan and Lea Daniel (Wright Group, Big Book and cassette)

"Goober Peas" - Alan and Lea Daniel (Wright Group, Big Book and cassette)

Direct Instruction: oo (ue, ew)

1. Make the "spooky sound" – o̅o̅-o̅o̅-o̅o̅. Ask the children if they know what letters stand for this sound. Help them to realize that several combinations of letters represent this sound: <u>oo, ew, ue, u-e</u> (June).

2. With their clipboards in hand, let the children search for words with these letter combinations. Use these words to make a chart. Classify the words according to spelling.

Unit VIII
Lesson 8

Working With Letters and Sounds

1. Ask the children to draw three adjacent squares called *soundboxes* on their chalkboards or papers.

2. Dictate these words: <u>blew</u>, <u>brew</u>, <u>flew</u>, <u>threw</u>, <u>grew</u>, <u>drew</u>, <u>crew</u>, <u>stew</u>.

threw

th	r	ew

blew

b	l	ew

Blend, Read and Write

1. Blend and read:

ūse   fūse   Jūne   tūne   blūe   trūe

2. Write: The bird flew away.

Word Construction

1. Ask the children to sort for the following letters (page 407):

<u>b</u>	l	e	w	<u>d</u>	c	h	t	r	f	<u>g</u>

2. Make the following words: <u>blew</u>, <u>drew</u>, <u>chew</u>, <u>blew</u>, <u>flew</u>, <u>threw</u>, <u>grew</u>, <u>crew</u>.

Book to Enhance Reading Comprehension, Skill and Language Development

Guided Reading:

<u>My Sister June</u> - Deborah Eaton (Modern Curriculum Press, <u>Ready Readers</u>)

"The Wishing Well" - Arnold Lobel (Houghton Mifflin, <u>Literary Readers, Book 1</u>)

Independent Reading:

Add beginner books that have been introduced to the class.

Writing Frame:

(Based on the story <u>Stellaluna</u>.)

The best part of <u>Stellaluna</u> was

_____

_____.

Make Your Own Little Books

<u>It's June</u>, pages 287-288. (Book 61)

Letter Cards for Word Construction (page 407)

Word Cards for Sentence Construction (Page 408)

"June, June, come soon," said Mrs. Smith. "I need a rest!"

8

It's June

Name _____

1

"It's true! It's true! I can go, too! I can see my gram!" said Maria.

6

"It's true! It's true!" yelled Jen. "Soon there will be no school. I can play ball with my friends."

3

"It's June! It's June,"
shouted Jessica. "Soon
there will be no school.
I can play all day!"

2

"June. I'll have
nothing to do. I can
just sit and look at
the moon," said Jill.

7

"June! I love June!
I can swim in my
pool," said Jon.

4

"No school in June!
Soon I will go to see
my gram," said Cris.

5

Unit VIII
Lesson 9

Sight Vocabulary:

- Introduce <u>ugly</u>, <u>lived</u>, <u>parents</u>, <u>because</u>, <u>picture</u>, <u>during</u>, <u>supposed</u>
- Phonics and Structural Analysis: /air/ <u>scare</u>, homophones (hair, hare) syllabication of two syllable words; contractions—wasn't, wouldn't, _ly (family)

Spelling: air, fair, hair, chair

Grammar, Mechanics and Usage:
Comparative adjectives (pretty, prettier, prettiest)

Developing Phonemic Awareness

Read Aloud:
<u>Pierre</u> - Maurice Sendak (Scholastic, <u>Literacy Place</u>)
<u>The Three Bears</u> - Paul Galdone (Seabury)
<u>Little Bear</u> - Else Holmelund Minarek (Harper Row)
<u>A Chair for My Mother</u> - Vera Williams (Greenwillow)
<u>Bears</u> - Ruth Krauss (Harper)

Shared Reading:
<u>Each Peach Pear Plum</u> - Janet and Allan Ahlberg (Viking)
<u>Oh, A-Hunting We Will Go</u> - John Langstaff (Houghton Mifflin, Big Book)

Rhymes and Poems:
"Pierre" - Maurice Sendak (Scholastic, <u>Literacy Place</u>)
"The Animal Fair" - Anonymous (<u>The Random House Book of Poetry for Children</u>)

Song:
"The Animal Fair" - Alan and Lea Daniel (Wright Group, Big Book and cassette)

Direct Instruction: /air/

1. Put the text of <u>Bears</u> by Ruth Krauss (Harper) on the overhead projector.

2. After reading it several times, ask the children to listen for words that rhyme with <u>hairs</u>. (How many <u>hairs</u> are on your head?) Read the rhyme again.

Tip:

The object of this spelling lesson is to introduce students to English variant spellings. The goal should <u>not</u> be mastery at this level.

Unit VIII
Lesson 9

3. Call on children to locate the rhyming words. Write the words on the board.

4. Lead the children to discover that the words <u>everywhere</u>, <u>bear</u> and <u>chair</u> all have the sound /air/ within them, only with different spellings.

5. Ask the children to help you locate words with the /air/ sound. Let children write these words on index cards. Use them to classify during center time.

Direct Instruction: syllabication of two syllable words

1. Start out by clapping once for one syllable words and twice for two syllable words. Review the difference between consonants and vowels.

2. Show the children how to decode the following words by first dividing them before the consonant _le.

     lit tle   bub ble   stum ble

3. Give the children practice in decoding these words:

ripple	fiddle	toddle	bottle
handle	spindle	dimple	cripple

Direct Instruction: homophones

1. Remind the children that English is considered to be a very difficult language to learn, partly because of the way words are spelled. Tell them that there are many clues that tell us the meaning of a word. Say, "For example 'hair' is spelled h-a-i-r, (write on board), but 'hare' is spelled h-a-r-e. How do we know which is which?" Help the children to see the importance of using context clues.

2. Write these sentences on the board or on a chart. Read and discuss their meanings. Look for key words.

Carol has brown <u>hair</u>.   The <u>hare</u> is like a rabbit.

I have a new <u>pair</u> of socks.   This <u>pear</u> tastes good.

He likes to look at the <u>bear</u> at the zoo.   Don't walk in <u>bare</u> feet.

Unit VIII
Lesson 9

3. Play a game of "Pears." Write sentences with common homophones on pear shaped pieces of paper. Pass them out to the children. Let them walk around the room until they've found their "pairs." Or, play a game like Old Maid ("Rotten Pear.")

I have brown <u>hair</u>.

A <u>hare</u> is like a rabbit.

Writing Frame:

(Retell the story of "The Three Bears.")

Once upon a time _____

_____.

One day _____.

Goldilocks _____.

At the end_____.

Working With Letters and Sounds

1. Write the word <u>air</u> in red on an index card. Tell the children that it represents one sound in the English language _/air/.

2. Show the children how to construct words by combining consonants (in black) with /air/.

| h | air |

3. With the children, construct the following words on the pocket chart or overhead projector: <u>chair</u>, <u>fair</u>, <u>hair</u>, <u>lair</u>, <u>pair</u>.

4. Do the same with: <u>stare</u>, <u>care</u>, <u>bare</u>, <u>mare</u>, <u>rare</u>, <u>scare</u>.

Blend, Read and Write

1. Blend and read:

| air | chair | fair | hair | pair |
| bare | care | dare | fare | hare |

2. Write: She takes care of her hair.

Unit VIII
Lesson 9

Books to Enhance Reading Comprehension, Skill and Language Development

Guided Reading:

The Not-So-Scary Scarecrow - Robin Bloksberg (Modern Curriculum Press, Ready Readers)

"Clyde Monster" - Robert L. Crowe (Houghton Mifflin, Literary Readers, Book 1)

Bears in the Night - Stan and Jan Berenstain (Random House)

The Three Billy Goats Gruff - Mark Thaler (Scholastic, Literacy Place)

Independent Reading:

Add easy books that have been introduced to the class.

Writing Frame:

My Pet

I have a [dog].

It [is brown and white].

I take care [of him].

I [give him a bath].

Make Your Own Little Books:

The Circus Bear, pages 293-294. (Book 62)

Word Cards for Sentence Construction (page 409)

Tip:

If the child doesn't have a pet, let him or her write about a class pet or an imaginary one.

62

anywhere!

8

The Circus Bear

Name _____

1

I like it when he
gives a scare.

6

I like it when he
combs his hair.

3

293
Reproducible

© Fearon Teacher Aids FE7948

I like to watch
the circus bear.

2

I like to watch the
circus bear . . .

7

I like it when he
holds the chair.

4

I like it when he
jumps off the stair.

5

294

Unit VIII
Lesson 10

Sight Vocabulary:

- Review <u>there</u>, <u>friends</u>, <u>any</u>, <u>from</u>, <u>where</u>, <u>work</u>, <u>little</u>, <u>Father</u>
- Introduce <u>every</u>, <u>pretty</u>, <u>because</u>, <u>picture</u>
- Phonics and Structural Analysis: /ô/ au, aw

Spelling: saw, jaw, raw, straw, cause, because, caught, dawn, lawn, fawn

Grammar, Mechanics and Usage:

Comparative adjectives <u>pretty</u>, <u>prettier</u>, <u>prettiest</u>; <u>ugly</u>, <u>uglier</u>, <u>ugliest</u>.

Developing Phonemic Awareness

Read Aloud:

<u>The Three Wishes</u> - Paul Galdone (McGraw Hill)

<u>The Princess and the Pea</u> - Hans Christian Andersen, illustrated by Dorothée Duntze. (North-South Books)

Shared Reading:

<u>Rumpelstiltskin</u> - Brenda Parkes (Rigby, Big Book)

<u>Jack and the Beanstalk</u> - Judith Smith (Rigby, Big Book)

<u>Bones, Bones, Bones , Dinosaur Bones</u> - Byron Barton (Scholastic, <u>Literacy Place</u>)

Rhymes and Poems:

"See-Saw, Margery Daw" - Mother Goose

"The Little Turtle" - Vachel Lindsay in <u>Sing a Song of Popcorn</u> (Scholastic)

"Auk Talk" - Mary Ann Hoberman in <u>The Raucous Auk</u> (Viking)

Song:

"And the Sidewalk Went All Around" (Wright Group, Big Book and Tape)

Direct instruction: /ô/ au, aw

1. Tell the children that today they will be learning about the sound represented by <u>au</u> and <u>aw</u>. Explain that you always think of these letters representing the "awesome" sound—because it is the sound people make when they see something great or wonderful:

<u>AW</u> - <u>AWESOME</u>.

Unit VIII
Lesson 10

2. Ask a "helper" to come up. Explain that you will say something and they are to respond with "AW - AWESOME!"

> Teacher: Look at the Grand Canyon!
> Child: Aw! Awesome!

Let pairs of students take turns making up "awesome" scenes.

3. Trace <u>au</u> and <u>aw</u> into the carpet while making the /ô/ sound.

Working With Letters and Sounds

1. Ask children to draw three adjacent squares called soundboxes on their chalkboards or papers.

2. Dictate the following words: <u>lawn</u>, <u>dawn</u>, <u>fawn</u>. Make sure the children understand that "aw" represents one phoneme.

lawn

Blend, Read and Write:

1. Blend and read.

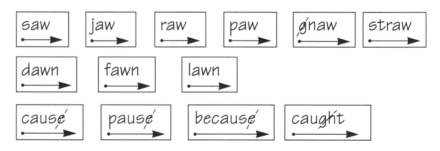

2. Write: I saw a little fawn.

Word Construction:

1. Ask the children to sort for the following letters (page 410):

2. Make the following words: <u>raw</u>, <u>saw</u>, <u>jaw</u>, <u>paw</u>, <u>lawn</u>, <u>dawn</u>, <u>fawn</u>.

Unit VIII Lesson 10

Books to Enhance Reading Comprehension, Skill and Language Development

Guided Reading:

"Clyde Monster" - Robert L. Crowe (Houghton Mifflin, <u>Literary Readers, Book 1</u>)

<u>Dinosaur Days</u> - Judy Nayer (Modern Curriculum Press, <u>Ready Readers</u>)

Independent Reading:

Add books already introduced to the class.

Make Your Own Little Books:

<u>The Lion and the Mouse</u>, pages 298-299. (Book 63)

Letter Cards for Word Construction (page 410)

Word Cards for Sentence Construction (page 411)

Evaluation: Unit VIII

Directions:

1. Ask each child to read the lists of words and the sentences.

List A	List B
pull	saw
who	thought
once	night
make	first
talk	were
through	buy
noise	many
every	because
during	lived
could	would

He lived there for a long time.
They were afraid of the dark.

2. Dictate: Last night I heard a loud noise.

63

Soon the lion was set free by the little mouse.

8

The Lion and the Mouse
adapted from Aesop

Name _____

1

✂ - ✂

Soon after that the lion got caught in a net. Some hunters wanted to take him to the zoo.

6

The lion grabbed the mouse and was just about to kill it.

3

A big lion was sleeping when a mouse came by him. The mouse hit the lion's jaw and woke him.

2

"Help me! Help me!" cried the lion. The mouse heard him. He ran to the lion and started to gnaw at the rope.

7

"Please let me go," begged the mouse. "And someday I will help you."

4

299
Reproducible

The lion laughed. "How can a little mouse like you help me?" But the lion let the mouse go.

5

Make your own words.

e	e	<u>b</u>	<u>s</u>
a	m		

Reproducible

Cut and arrange to make sentences. Don't forget the period.

I	see	the
bee		
I	see	the
I	see	the
I	see	the

Reproducible

301

Make your own words.

c	t	a	<u>s</u>
<u>b</u>	e	e	<u>s</u>

Reproducible   © Fearon Teacher Aids FE7948

Cut and arrange to make sentences. Don't forget the period.

I	see	the
red	bird	like
yellow	blue	green
dog	crayon	tree
wagon	cat	bicycle

Reproducible

Make your own words.

e	<u>b</u>	m	<u>s</u>
e	a	t	c

Reproducible

© Fearon Teacher Aids FE7948

Cut and arrange to make sentences. Don't forget the period.

I	the	see
cat	bee	bat
is	black	The
sat	mat	red

Reproducible

Make your own words.

a	<u>n</u>	t	c
m	't	o	e
e	<u>b</u>	<u>s</u>	N

Cut and arrange to make sentences. Don't forget the period.

A	An	ant
black	is	I
see	mat	the
The	tan	red
can	can't	

　Reproducible

Make your own words.

o	a	<u>b</u>	c
m	t	T	M
<u>n</u>	e	e	<u>s</u>

Cut and arrange to make sentences. Don't forget the period.

I	can	not
see	a	cat
man	Mom	The
is	on	the
mat		

Reproducible

Make your own words.

a	<u>b</u>	c	<u>d</u>
m	<u>n</u>	o	<u>s</u>
e	e	t	D
N	M		

No	I	can
not	see	Dad
is	on	the
sand	a	cat
and	Mom	seem
mad	sad	

Reproducible

Make your own words.

a	<u>b</u>	c	<u>d</u>
e	e	f	m
<u>n</u>	s	t	o
M	D	N	

Cut and arrange to make sentences. Don't forget the period.

Mom	can	feed
the	cat	I
need	a	fan
No	I	can't
feed	fat	man

Reproducible

313

Make your own words.

a	<u>b</u>	c	<u>d</u>
e	e	f	m
<u>n</u>	o	<u>p</u>	<u>s</u>
t			

Cut and arrange to make sentences. Don't forget the period.

I'm	not	said
said	Mom	mad
Dad	fat	nap
can	I	pat
cat	black	pot
see	like	

Make your own words.

a	<u>b</u>	c	<u>d</u>
e	e	f	l
m	<u>n</u>	o	<u>p</u>
<u>s</u>	t		

Reproducible

Cut and arrange to make sentences. Don't forget the period.

I	like	to
see	Mom	and
Dad	feed	the
cat	A	man
is	on	a
lap	nap	sat

Reproducible

317

Make your own words.

a	<u>b</u>	c	<u>d</u>
e	e	f	l
m	<u>n</u>	o	P
r	<u>s</u>	t	R

© Fearon Teacher Aids FE7948

Cut and arrange to make sentences. Don't forget the period.

I	man	a
see	can	The
deer	of	beans
Ron	Ann	fast
and	ran	rat

Reproducible

Make your own words.

a	<u>b</u>	c	<u>d</u>
e	e	f	i
l	m	<u>n</u>	o
<u>p</u>	r	<u>s</u>	t

© Fearon Teacher Aids FE7948

It	like	an
looked	a	but
it	wasn't	a
an	cat	dog
pig	bat	bee
deer		

Make your own words.

a	<u>b</u>	c	<u>d</u>
e	e	f	h
i	l	m	<u>n</u>
o	<u>p</u>	r	<u>s</u>
t			

Reproducible

Cut and arrange to make sentences. Don't forget the period.

Dad	a	red
has	cap	His
hat	is	black
The	has	hat
his	on	cat
hot	ham	hand
on	his	

Make your own words.

a	<u>b</u>	c	<u>d</u>
e	e	f	g
l	m	<u>n</u>	o
<u>p</u>	r	<u>s</u>	t
<u>h</u>	i		

Dad	a	pig
got	big	dog
black	can	go
to	sand	dig
in	the	The
man	see	

Make your own words.

a	<u>b</u>	c	<u>d</u>
e	e	f	g
i	k	l	m
<u>n</u>	o	<u>p</u>	r
<u>s</u>	t		

Cut and arrange to make sentences. Don't forget the period.

Mom	are	not
and	in	the
Dad	sand	hot
It	in	sink
is	the	like
pink	sad	mask

Reproducible

Make your own words.

a	<u>b</u>	c	<u>d</u>
e	e	f	g
h	i	k	l
m	<u>n</u>	o	<u>p</u>
r	<u>s</u>	t	

Cut and arrange to make sentences. Don't forget the period.

I	to	the
like	bike	hide
ride	likes	Tom
the	cat	hike
and	Ann	

Reproducible

Make your own words.

w	k	b	m
h	p	e	e
s			

Reproducible   © Fearon Teacher Aids FE7948

Cut and arrange to make sentences. Don't forget the period.

We	a	week
will	in	He
go	can	me
see	I	saw
the	tree	green
wig	red	yellow
and	black	bee

Make your own words.

e	t	<u>n</u>	<u>d</u>
r	T	<u>b</u>	<u>s</u>
m	B		

© Fearon Teacher Aids FE7948

Cut and arrange to make sentences. Don't forget the period.

Ted	a	saw
man	met	ten
has	pets	feed
Ann	the	dog
Mom	a	has
pen	red	led
get	I	can

Reproducible

333

Make your own words.

<u>b</u>	a	c	l
t	g	r	o
<u>d</u>			

Reproducible   © Fearon Teacher Aids FE7948

Cut and arrange to make sentences. Don't forget the period.

I	boat	coat
saw	The	is
a	red	won't
the	go	goat
will	on	not
You	get	No

Reproducible

335

Make your own words.

x	<u>b</u>	o	f
a	M	i	m
<u>s</u>	t	w	

Reproducible

© Fearon Teacher Aids FE7948

Cut and arrange to make sentences. Don't forget the period.

Max	a	box
has	The	is
red	of	seeds
fox	the	saw
man	I	mix
A	pen	in

Cut and arrange to make sentences. Don't forget the period.

Jill	will	ride
bikes	and	hide
Bill	go	jet
on	a	get
jam	can	of
to	hill	big

338

Reproducible

© Fearon Teacher Aids FE7948

y	e	s	t
b	m	w	s
n	j		

Yes	saw	did
I	No	see
jet	big	can't
get	the	ride
on	pet	I'm
is	wet	get
dog	cat	man

Make your own words.

a	v	<u>b</u>	c
<u>n</u>	f	D	m
N	t	<u>p</u>	

Reproducible

341

Cut and arrange to make sentences. Don't forget the period.

have	of	I
lot	a	love
you	for	to
The	ran	An
man	get	ant
can	it	go

Reproducible

Make your own words.

z	o	o	t
i	p	l	f
m	n		

Reproducible

Cut and arrange to make sentences. Don't forget the period.

we	You	the
will	to	zoo
go	soon	too
moon	I	am
saw	going	zap
bee	We	Bill

Reproducible

© Fearon Teacher Aids FE7948

Make your own words.

q	<u>u</u>	i	l
<u>s</u>	R	l	w
t	k	<u>p</u>	c
k			

Cut and arrange to make sentences. Don't forget the period.

feel	I	too
sick	am	It
quick	is	not
can't	it	Can
kick	you	the
ball	saw	You

Make your own words.

<u>u</u>	c	t	<u>n</u>
f	<u>s</u>	<u>b</u>	r
m			

Reproducible   **347**

Cut and arrange to make sentences. Don't forget the period.

put	the	I
They	nuts	can
in	cup	up
go	in	jet
a	It	to
is	run	fun

Reproducible

© Fearon Teacher Aids FE7948

Make your own words.

t	h	i	<u>s</u>
e	m	<u>n</u>	w
k	a	t	

Reproducible

Cut and arrange to make sentences. Don't forget the period.

Reproducible

I	to	the
want	go	to
zoo	Do	you
too	come	me
with	don't	I'll
put	here	it

Reproducible

© Fearon Teacher Aids FE7948

Make your own words.

<u>s</u>	h	t	<u>p</u>
i	o	w	f
e	e	<u>d</u>	

351

Reproducible

Cut and arrange to make sentences. Don't forget the period.

will	hello	to
I	say	him
It	is	good
make	wish	dish
a	like	for
fish	pets	are

c	h	i	o
p	k	r	s
t	n	a	e
e			

Cut and arrange to make sentences. Don't forget the period.

I	want	lunch
don't	to	was
have	good	Mom
made	a	He
at	peek	will
me	come	and

© Fearon Teacher Aids FE7948

Make your own words.

h	w	<u>n</u>	e
t	m	h	<u>d</u>
p	k	<u>b</u>	K
B			

Reproducible

355

Cut and arrange to make sentences. Don't forget the period.

When	he	to
will	come	see
us	Ken	Hello
said	me	The
men	at	ten
went	the	zoo

Make your own words.

l	k	t	<u>b</u>
r	c	<u>n</u>	h
<u>s</u>	h	o	o

Reproducible

357

Cut and arrange to make sentences. Don't forget the period.

I	look	at
Look	will	the
It	a	good
is	book	like
What	you	do
want	to	do

c	a	k	e
<u>b</u>	<u>s</u>	m	t
f			

359

Cut and arrange to make sentences. Don't forget the period.

I	make	good
can	a	cake
My	is	name
the	same	want
What	you	take
do	to	zoo

Reproducible

Make your own words.

<u>b</u>	t	m	<u>n</u>
f	<u>s</u>	h	w
e	a		

Reproducible

361

Cut and arrange to make sentences. Don't forget the period.

He	to	beach
goes	the	likes
to	me	not
eats	heat	take
this	a	good
seat	peach	meat

© Fearon Teacher Aids FE7948

m	s̲	d̲	l
w	p̲	h	a
y			

Cut and arrange to make sentences. Don't forget the period.

Today	can	with
we	play	Jill
good	to	the
go	zoo	Mom
for	will	May
pay	it	got

Reproducible

Cut apart and make into compound words.

in	to
my	self
some	thing
some	day
him	self
some	one

Reproducible

Cut and arrange to make sentences. Don't forget the period.

He	to	the
goes	see	big
at	cats	zoo
I	dogs	fish
like	and	go
Someday	want	will

Make your own words.

f	t	c	<u>n</u>
h	<u>b</u>	o	r

Reproducible

367

Cut and arrange to make sentences. Don't forget the period.

I	one	for
more	want	him
go	north	the
to	short	will
cut	take	This
is	my	mom

<u>n</u>	c	<u>b</u>	<u>d</u>
t	r	f	h
o	w		

Cut and arrange to make sentences. Don't forget the period.

We	milk	a
get	from	cow
Do	know	how
you	we	It
comes	will	it
I	do	now

Reproducible   © Fearon Teacher Aids FE7948

Make your own words.

h	o	e	p
v	l	m	n
t			

Reproducible

Cut and arrange to make sentences. Don't forget the period.

Soon	will	home
come	Dad	I
Mom	me	must
woke	up	go
now	when	When
he	it	broke

Reproducible

r	<u>n</u>	m	<u>p</u>
<u>b</u>	r	<u>s</u>	t
<u>d</u>	a	i	

Cut and arrange to make sentences. Don't forget the period.

can	We	train
take	other	want
the	one	too
I	is	good
know	it's	It's
It	will	rain

374

Make your own words.

y	m	t	r
f	l	<u>d</u>	w
<u>s</u>	h		

Cut and arrange to make sentences. Don't forget the period.

your	this	pet
Is	dog	cat
brown	Why	that
did	do	I
he	will	try
not	cry	it

© Fearon Teacher Aids FE7948

Make your own words.

r	t	<u>b</u>	<u>n</u>
f	l	<u>d</u>	c
c	g	h	e
w			

Reproducible

377

Cut and arrange to make sentences. Don't forget the period.

My	makes	stew
mom	good	Do
you	how	to
know	make	your
it	flew	in
jet	a	I

Make your own words.

k	i	t	e
b̲	r	d̲	h
q	u̲	w	s̲

Reproducible

379

Cut and arrange to make sentences. Don't forget the period.

I	like	know
would	to	how
to	make	a
cake	plane	one
more	thing	kite
ride	my	bike

© Fearon Teacher Aids FE7948

Make your own words.

<u>u</u>	<u>b</u>	f	<u>n</u>
r	l	m	c
t	J	<u>p</u>	h
<u>s</u>	t		

Cut and arrange to make sentences. Don't forget the period.

I	one	thing
want	more	cat
The	is	hot
sun	too	today
Your	wants	to
mother	you	come

c	<u>b</u>	k	<u>d</u>
h	<u>p</u>	m	f
a	r		

Cut and arrange to make sentences. Don't forget the period.

Do	want	is
you	to	the
go	park	Can
bark	a	Don't
like	dog	harm
Mark	it	here

Reproducible © Fearon Teacher Aids FE7948

Make your own words.

f	<u>n</u>	<u>d</u>	h
r	<u>s</u>	<u>b</u>	g
t	o	<u>u</u>	m
e			

Reproducible

385

Cut and arrange to make sentences. Don't forget the period.

There's	more	on
one	thing	the
I	ground	will
it	pick	up
hound	dog	want
a	no	sound

Make your own words.

f	c	e	r
p	l	m	n
i	s	a	

Reproducible

Cut and arrange to make sentences. Don't forget the period.

think	I	are
mice	nice	Where
the	did	take
race	place	jumping
was	with	him
help	Dad	The

Reproducible

Make your own words.

<u>b</u>	l	l	c
a	w	f	h
m	<u>s</u>	t	

Cut and arrange to make sentences. Don't forget the period.

called	from	Mom
My	father	Do
work	you	any
have	balls	Can
for	find	me
call	I	will

390

Make your own words.

<u>s</u>	i	<u>n</u>	g
w	r	<u>b</u>	k
t	h		

Cut and arrange to make sentences. Don't forget the period.

Bring	to	Go
it	me	get
that	thing	is
I	want	come
my	to	play
friends	ring	where

© Fearon Teacher Aids FE7948

c	a	k	e
<u>b</u>	l	t	r
q	<u>u</u>	f	<u>s</u>
h			

Cut and arrange to make sentences. Don't forget the period.

The	red	said
little	hen	Who
will	me	I
help	bake	home
this	cake	take
eat	bread	this

© Fearon Teacher Aids FE7948

Make your own words.

b	o	l	d
f	g	h	m
s	t	c	

upon	a	was
Once	time	a
there	little	man
old	He	go
could	again	get
gold	it	sold

Reproducible   © Fearon Teacher Aids FE7948

Make your own words.

<u>s</u>	q	<u>u</u>	i
e	a	k	r
t	e	l	z
<u>n</u>	<u>s</u>	h	

Reproducible

I	walking	mice
went	was	went
talking	The	squeak
Don't	the	bread
squish	will	you
squirt	home	am

Make your own words.

<u>s</u>	<u>u</u>	<u>n</u>	<u>n</u>
y	<u>b</u>	f	t
t	i	l	l

399

Cut and arrange to make sentences. Don't forget the period.

Once	my	was
I	saw	very
teacher	happy	her
to	see	talked
She	a	fun
had	puppy	It

Reproducible

© Fearon Teacher Aids FE7948

Make your own words.

l	c	t	R
<u>n</u>	<u>s</u>	o	i
<u>b</u>	r	<u>p</u>t	f
y			

Reproducible

Cut and arrange to make sentences. Don't forget the period.

I	a	has
know	boy	good
who	toy	like
to	talk	with
park	the	went
through	zoo	She

Reproducible

© Fearon Teacher Aids FE7948

<u>b</u>	r	i	g
h	t	<u>s</u>	r
l	m	<u>n</u>	t
f			

Cut and arrange to make sentences. Don't forget the period.

I	boy	one
thought	had	Once
every	like	toy
this	a	fight
with	It	right
is	not	to

© Fearon Teacher Aids FE7948

Make your own words.

f   i   r   <u>s</u>

t   <u>d</u>   <u>b</u>   h

Reproducible

Cut and arrange to make sentences. Don't forget the period.

thought	The	bird
girl	she	saw
and	boy	the
were	first	it
to	see	buy
do	every	day

Reproducible

Make your own words.

<u>b</u>	l	e	w
<u>d</u>	c	h	t
r	f	g	

Reproducible   **407**

Cut and arrange to make sentences. Don't forget the period.

was	in	June
born	He	blue
I	the	like
sky	bread	to
sing	chew	gum
tune	many	things

Reproducible

Cut and arrange to make sentences. Don't forget the period.

hair	prettier	way
looks	My	this
The	is	ugly
chair	I	scare
wouldn't	you	He
wasn't	home	good

Reproducible

Make your own words.

f	<u>s</u>	a	w
<u>p</u>	l	<u>d</u>	<u>n</u>
j	r		

Reproducible   © Fearon Teacher Aids FE7948

The	was	in
lion	the	hit
caught	A	saw
net	mouse	He
his	gnawed	on
jaw	rope	free

Recommended Supplementary Books and Materials

Rigby Big Books—I don't know what I'd do without these beautifully illustrated books. The print is large, color coded and easy for children to read. Available from Rigby, P.O. Box 797 Crystal Lake, IL. (1-800-822-8661)

Rigby Literacy 2000—These leveled books from Rigby provide the teacher with many little books for guided and independent reading.

Ready Readers—These books from Modern Curriculum Press are unique because they provide practice with phonetically regular words without sacrificing the natural flow of language. Available from Modern Curriculum Press, 299 Jefferson Road, P.O. Box 480, Parsippany, NJ 07054-8655. (1-800-321-3106)

Nellie Edge Big Books and Tapes—These inexpensive materials are designed to teach reading skills "within the context of meaningful language." Each Big Book comes with a Little Book that can be copied and sent home with children. Available from Nellie Edge Resources, P.O. Box 12399, Salem, OR 97309-0399. (1-800-523-4591)

Wright Group Books and Tapes—Is there a classroom in California without <u>Mrs. Wishy-Washy</u>? These delightful books captivate the interest of beginning readers everywhere. Available from The Wright Group, 19201 120th Avenue NE, Bothell, WA 98011. (1-800-823-2371)

Magnetic Letters and Tiles—These are great for word construction. Available at any toy or teacher supply store.

Raffi Tapes, Records and Books—Children love Raffi and will soon know his songs and books by heart. Available at all teacher supply stores.

Greg and Steve Records and Cassettes—These songs are very popular with children. Available at all teacher supply stores.

Living Books—If you don't have a computer and this wonderful software, beg, borrow or use your own money to get them for your classroom. Available from Random House, P.O. Box 6144, Novata, CA 94948-6144. (415-382-7818)

Mother Goose Rhymes—Two great resources for Mother Goose rhymes are: <u>The Real Mother Goose</u> Chicago, IL: Rand McNally, 1982 and <u>Tomie dePaola's Mother Goose</u> New York: G.P. Putnam's Sons, 1985.

Bibliography

Adams, Marilyn Jager. <u>Beginning to Read</u>. Cambridge: MIT, 1995.

Ashton-Warner, Sylvia. <u>Teacher</u>. New York: Simon and Schuster, 1963.

Bolton, Faye and Diane Snowball. <u>Ideas for Spelling</u>. Portsmouth: Heinemann, 1993.

Clay, Marie M. <u>The Early Detection of Reading Difficulties</u>. Third Edition. Portsmouth: Heinemann, 1985 and 1986.

Cunningham, Patricia. <u>Making Words</u>. Torrance, CA: Good Apple, 1994.

Delpit, Lisa, <u>Other People's Children</u>. New York: The New Press, 1995.

Fountas, Irene C. and Gay Su Pinnell. <u>Guided Reading</u>. Portsmouth: Heinemann, 1995.

Holdoway, D. <u>The Foundations of Literacy</u>. Sydney, Australia: Ashton Scholastic, 1979.

Hunter, Madeleine. <u>Mastery Teaching</u>. El Segundo, CA: Tip Publications, 1983.

Share, D. and Stanovich, K. "Cognitive Processes in Early Reading Development: Accommodating Individual Differences into a Mode of Acquisition." <u>Issues in Education: Contributions from Educational Psychology, Vol. 1</u> (1995), pp. 1-57.

Shefelbine, J. <u>Learning and Using Phonics in Beginning Reading</u>. New York: Scholastic, Inc., 1995.

<u>Teaching Reading</u>. Sacramento: California Department of Education, 1996.

Yopp, H. "Developing Phonemic Awareness in Young Children." <u>The Reading Teacher</u>, Vol. 45 (1992), pp. 696-703

Glossary of Terms

Compound word—A compound word is one that has been formed by putting two words together. Each part of the compound word should retain its original meaning. For example, "blackboard" and "something" are compound words but "butterfly" is not.

Consonant blend—A consonant blend consists of two or more letters blended together to represent sounds in a word. For example, st, str, bl, and br are all consonant blends.

Consonant digraph—A consonant digraph consists of two consonants to represent one sound. Ch, wh, sh and th are digraphs. Each digraph is a single phoneme.

Diphthong—A diphthong is a single sound (phoneme) made by two combined vowels. Oi, au and oy are diphthongs.

Decodable text—Text that a student can read by himself or herself, using the word attack strategies he or she has learned.

Decode—This term refers to reading words correctly; to convert the written symbols to the oral sounds they represent.

Encode—To encode is to transcribe an oral message into writing.

Grapheme—A written symbol that represents a sound made in speech. The grapheme b represents the sound heard at the beginning of the word ball.

Guided reading—This term refers to small group reading instruction, where the teacher teaches the child at his or her instructional level. The instruction usually involves the reading of an entire selection, but can focus on any skill or strategy that the teacher deems appropriate.

Instructional level—The child's instructional level is generally believed to be text that he or she can read with 90% accuracy.

Modeled reading—In modeled reading the teacher reads aloud, verbalizing her thinking strategies as she goes along. For example, he might say "Let's see, what do I think will happen next? Well, the lion's cage has been unlocked, so I think he might escape. Let's see if I'm right."

Modeled writing—The teacher writes in front of the children, explaining himself as he moves along. For example, "I'll begin by telling the reader what I'm going to write about" or "I'll use a question mark, since my character asked a question."

Morpheme—A morpheme is the smallest meaningful part of a word. The word hat has one morpheme, hats has two because the "s" conveys meaning (more than one).

Phoneme—A phoneme is the smallest unit of sound in a language. The word "chat" is comprised of three phonemes /ch/-/a/-/t/. The English language has approximately 44 phonemes.

Phonemic awareness—Phonemic awareness refers to recognizing sounds within words. A child who has "phonemic awareness" understands that the spoken word "cat" is represented by the phonemes /c/-/a/-/t/. Research tells us that this understanding is crucial to learning to read.

Orthography—This word refers to correct spelling or to the study of spelling.

Phonetics—Phonetics is the branch of linguistics that studies the sounds of a language (how the sounds are made, changed, represented in written form, etc.)

Phonics—Reading instruction that teaches the child the relationship between printed symbols and the sounds they represent.

Phonogram—A phonogram is a common word ending, such as all in ball, call, gall, hall, mall and small. Such words are also referred to as "word families" or "rimes."

Schwa—The schwa sound represents the diminished sound of any vowel in an unstressed syllable. For example, the first "a" in again is a schwa, which is represented by this symbol: ə.

Shared reading—Shared reading refers to the act of reading together, often between teacher and children, but can be a joint activity of more people of any age. The purpose is to give support to the novice reader.

Shared writing—Shared writing, like shared reading, means writing together.

Sight word—A word that is instantly recognized by the reader. In beginning reading it refers to a word that is not phonetically regular, such as "through."

"Temporary" spelling—This term (preferred over "invented" spelling by many teachers) refers to the beginning stages of spelling development in the young child.

Vowel combinations—A combination is a team of two vowels together that represent a long or short vowel sound. For example, ee, ea, ao, and ie are vowel combinations.

Word List for Beginners

I	make	he	ride	there	that
am	made	go	be	out	then
the	each	pig	me	about	than
red	was	are	we	where	their
like	day	asked	he	little	long
see	may	number	saw	many	who
a	way	one	you	find	time
at	play	two	get	all	very
no	some	or	will	called	boy
is	more	more	have	us	walk
so	and	for	ran	but	water
cat	of	know	too	must	happy
can	to	down	zoo	do	funny
not	as	now	up	put	were
on	if	how	they	come	her
she	into	other	just	here	first
when	his	your	would	want	air
which	had	my	could	with	use
what	has	by	from	don't	been
look	him	new	part	this	

44 Phonemes of English

(Linguists don't agree on the number of phonemes, but this is the number I use. When you see / / around a letter, it indicates that the sound should be said, not the name of the letter.)

ă	(apple)	/b/	(ball)	/g/	(goat)	/h/	(house)
ē	(elephant)	/f/	(fish)	/k/	(kite)	/l/	(love)
ĭ	(igloo)	/j/	(jack o'lantern)	ŏ	(octopus)	/p/	(pig)
/m/	(Mom)	/n/	(nut)	/t/	(table)	ŭ	(umbrella)
/r/	(rabbit)	/s/	(sun)	/y/	(yo-yo)	/z/	(zebra)
/v/	(violin)	/w/	(water)	/ch/	(chair)	/hw/	(wheel)
/sh/	(sheep)	/th/	(three)	ī	(ice)	ō	(oats)
ā	(ape)	ē	(eat)	ô	(saw)	/ou/	(out)
ū	(unicorn)	/oi/	(oil)	o͝o	(book)	oo	(moon)
/er/	(hurt)	/or/	(corn)	/air/	(chair)	är	(far)
ū	(use)	/ng/	(ring)	/d/	(dog)	/zh/	(vision)

© Fearon Teacher Aids FE7948

Name_____

Readiness Checklist

Letter names:

Aa ____	Bb ____	Cc ____	Dd ____
Ee ____	Ff ____	Gg ____	Hh ____
Ii ____	Jj ____	Kk ____	Ll ____
Mm ____	Nn ____	Oo ____	Pp ____
Qq ____	Rr ____	Ss ____	Tt ____
Uu ____	Vv ____	Ww ____	Xx ____
Yy ____	Zz ____		

Color words:

red ____   blue ____   yellow ____   green____

Rhyming words: Give me a word that rhymes with . . .

cat ____   ham ____   Jill ____   bell ____   it ____   make____

Consonant sounds:

b ____	k ____	d ____	f ____	g ____	h ____
q ____	r ____	l ____	m ____	n ____	p ____
y ____	z ____	s ____	t ____	v ____	w ____
c ____	j ____				

What's the Word?

1. Start again at the beginning of the sentence.

2. Skip the word and read to the end of the sentence.

3. Look at the unknown words. Blend the sounds of the letters together. Does the word make sense?

4. Try again.

Let's Begin Our Day

This is on a classroom chart used at the beginning of each day.

1. Who will be the president?
2. Who will take the roll?
3. Who will record the date and the weather?
4. Who will take the roll sheet to the office?
5. Who will find the surprise?
6. Who will get the mail?
7. Who will read the news?
8. Who wants to share?